creatures real and imagined

And a bunch of other stuff in a coloring book for old children

illustrated by
marlaena shannon

www.marlaena.com ISBN: 978-1519615862

CREATURES
REAL
and
IMAGINED

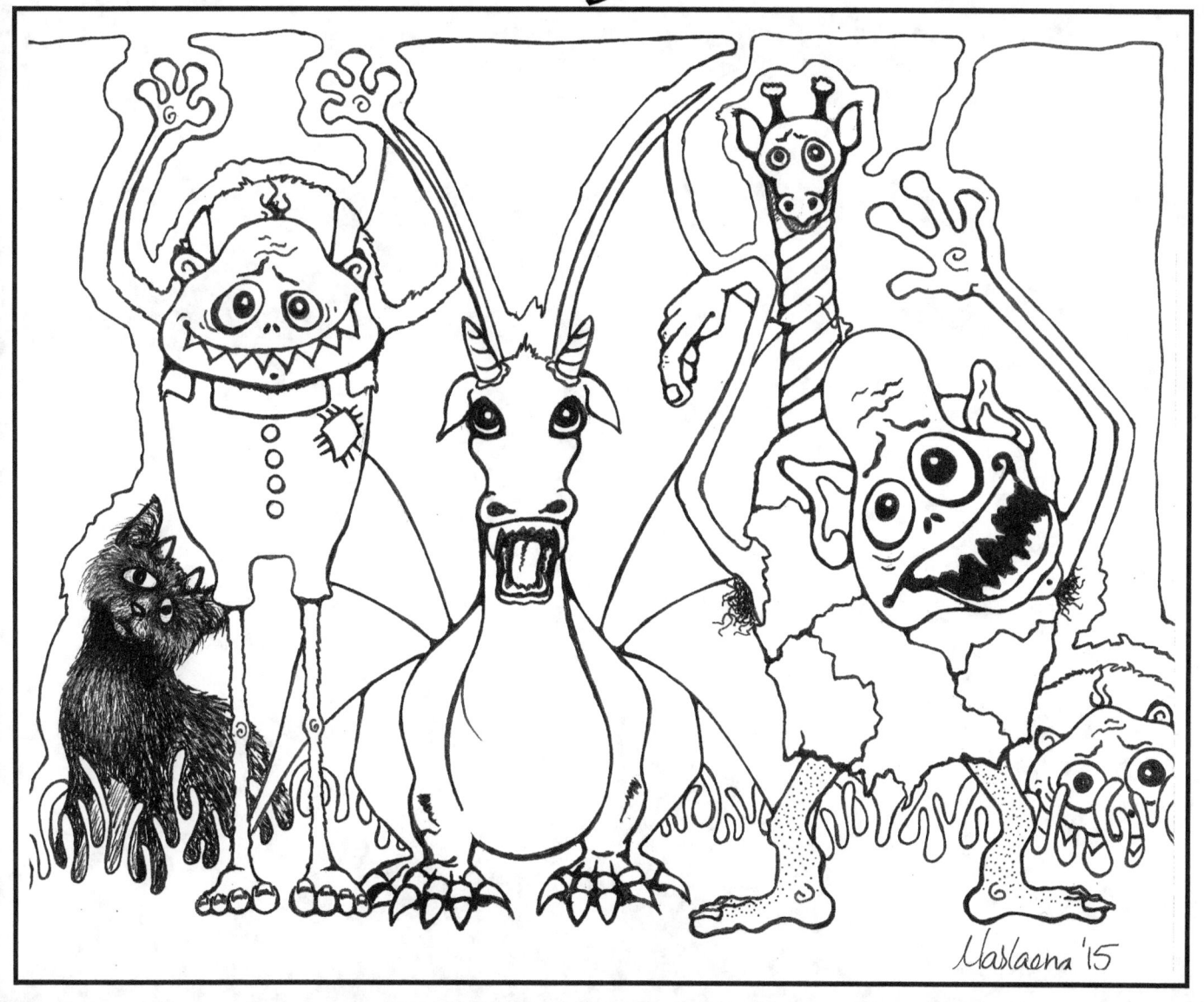

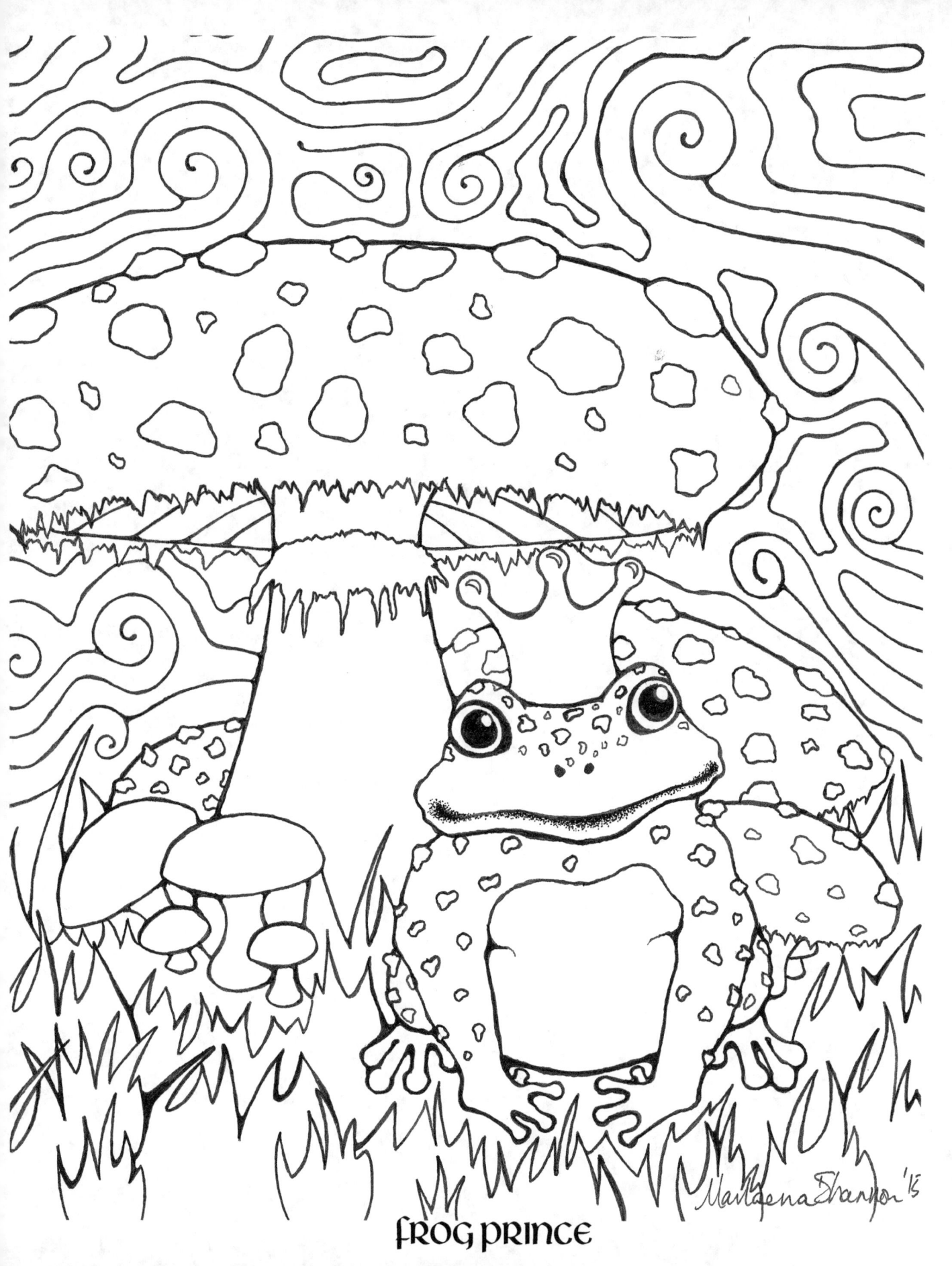

frog prince

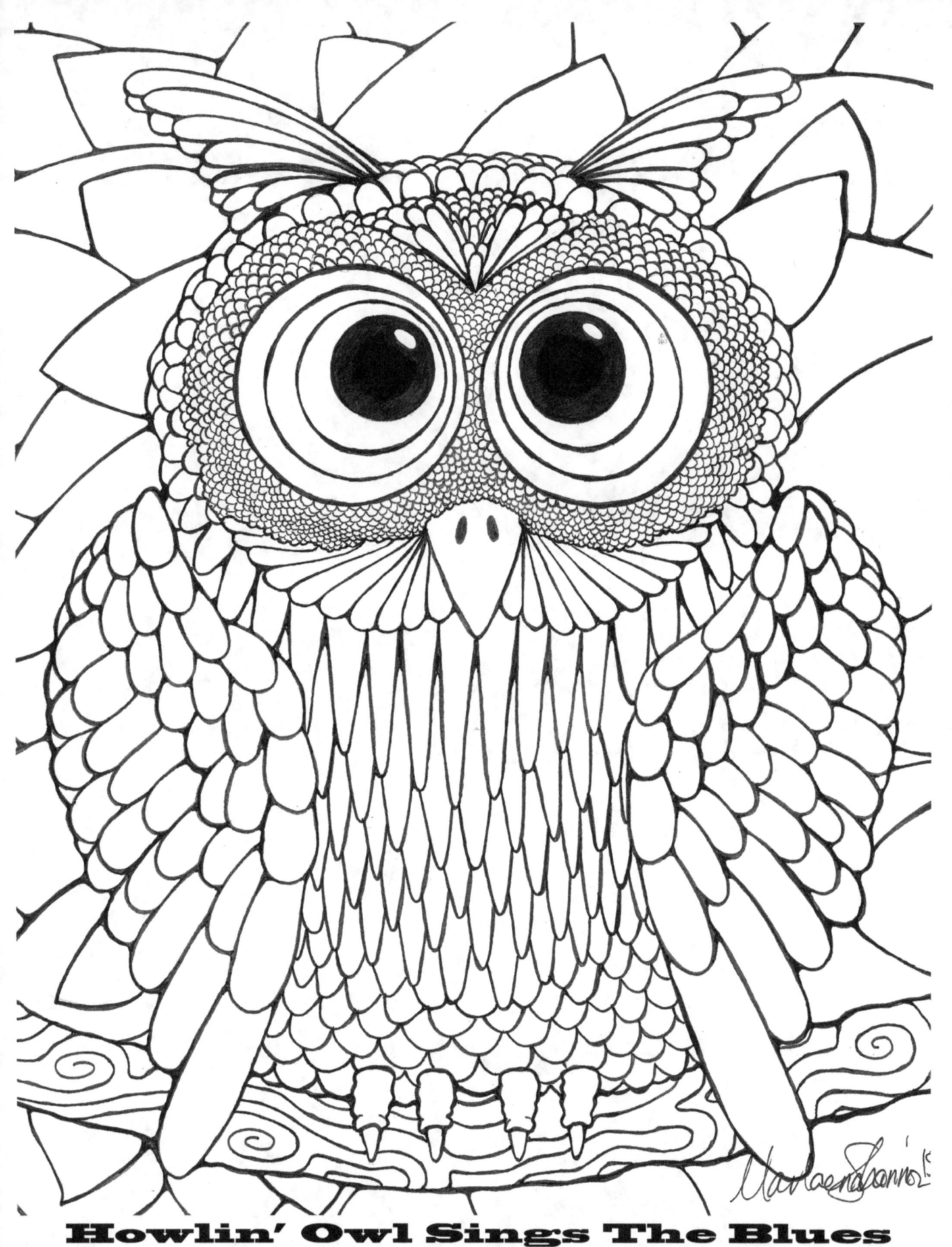

Howlin' Owl Sings The Blues

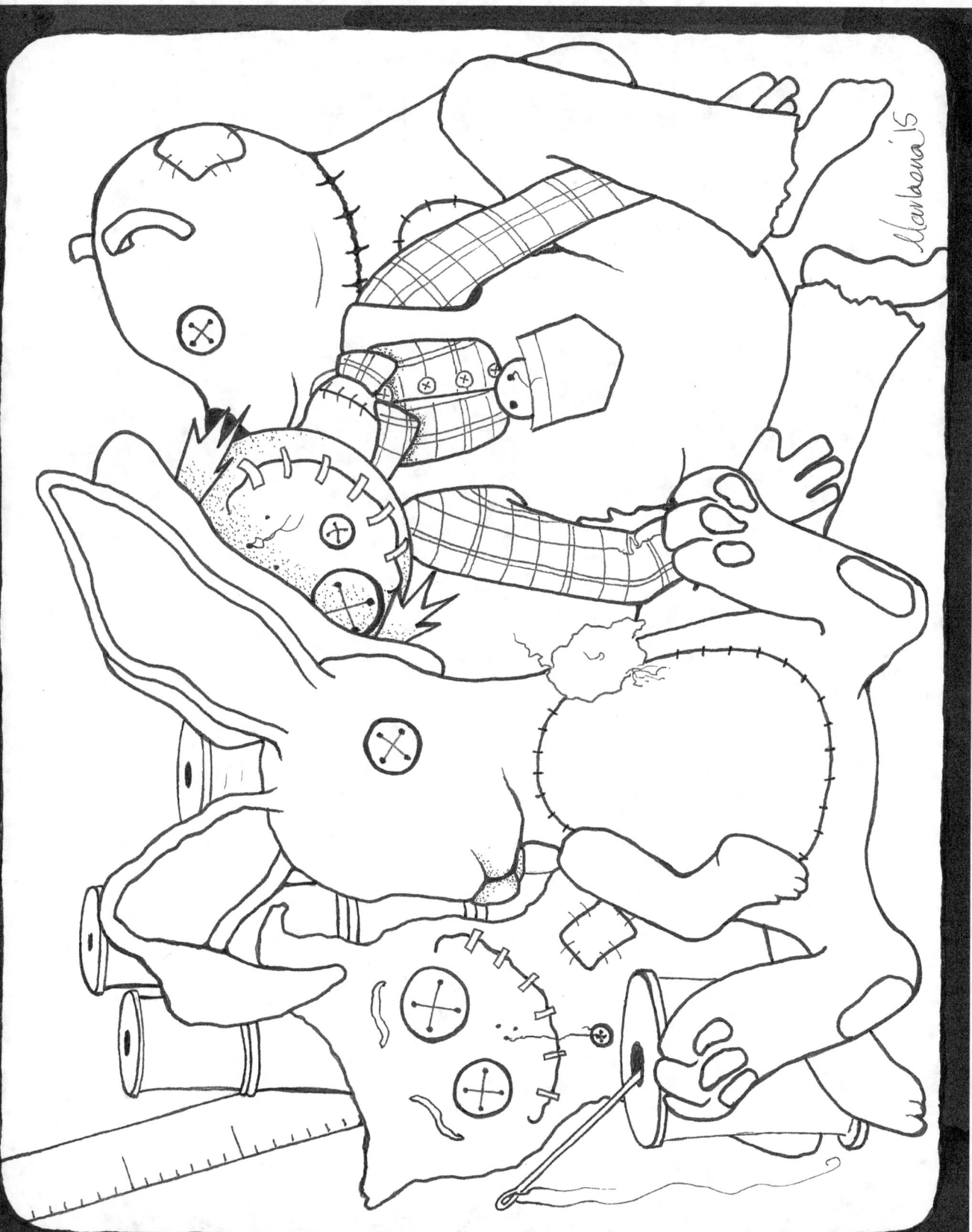

Bunny Learns To Sew

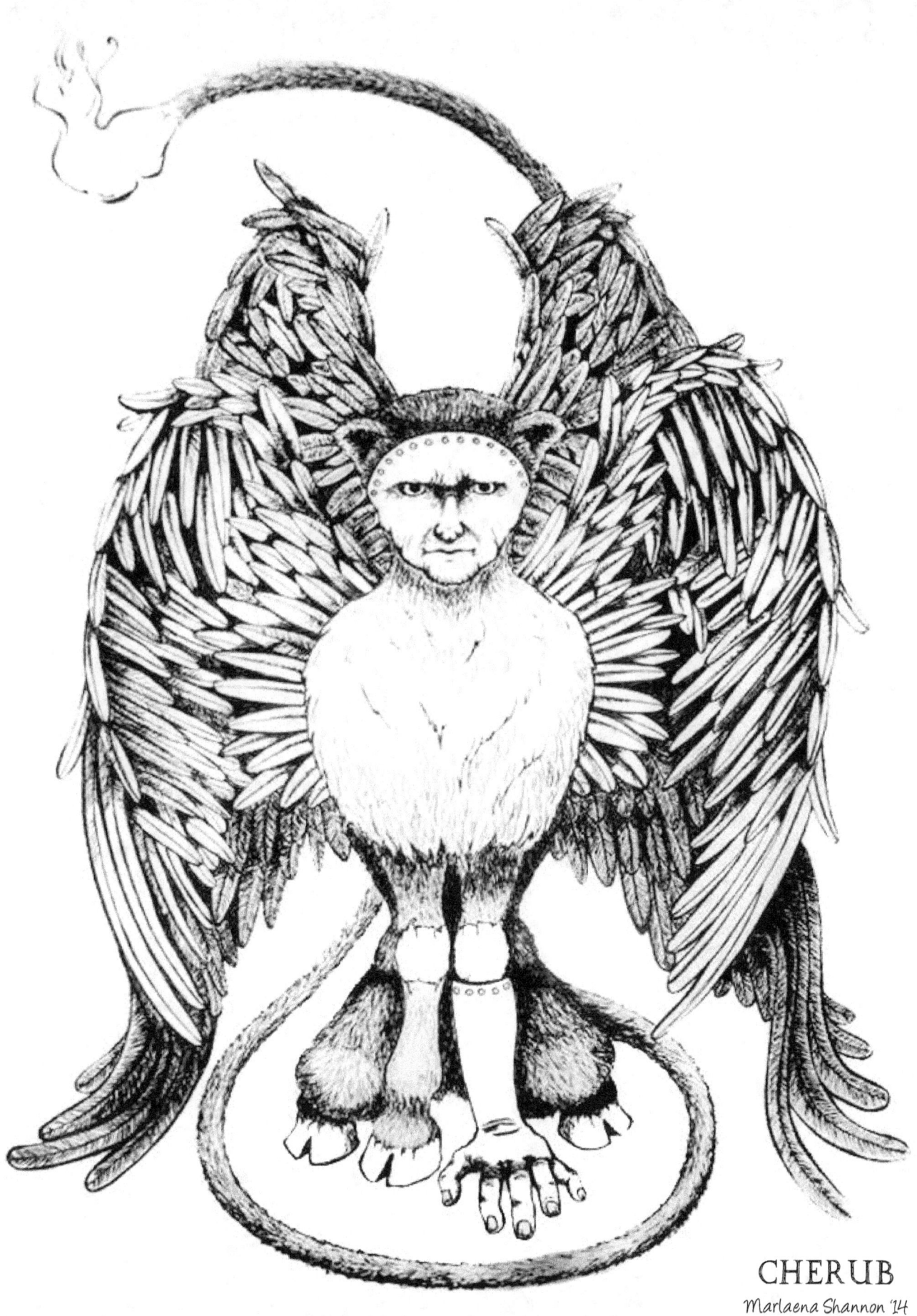

CHERUB

Marlaena Shannon '14

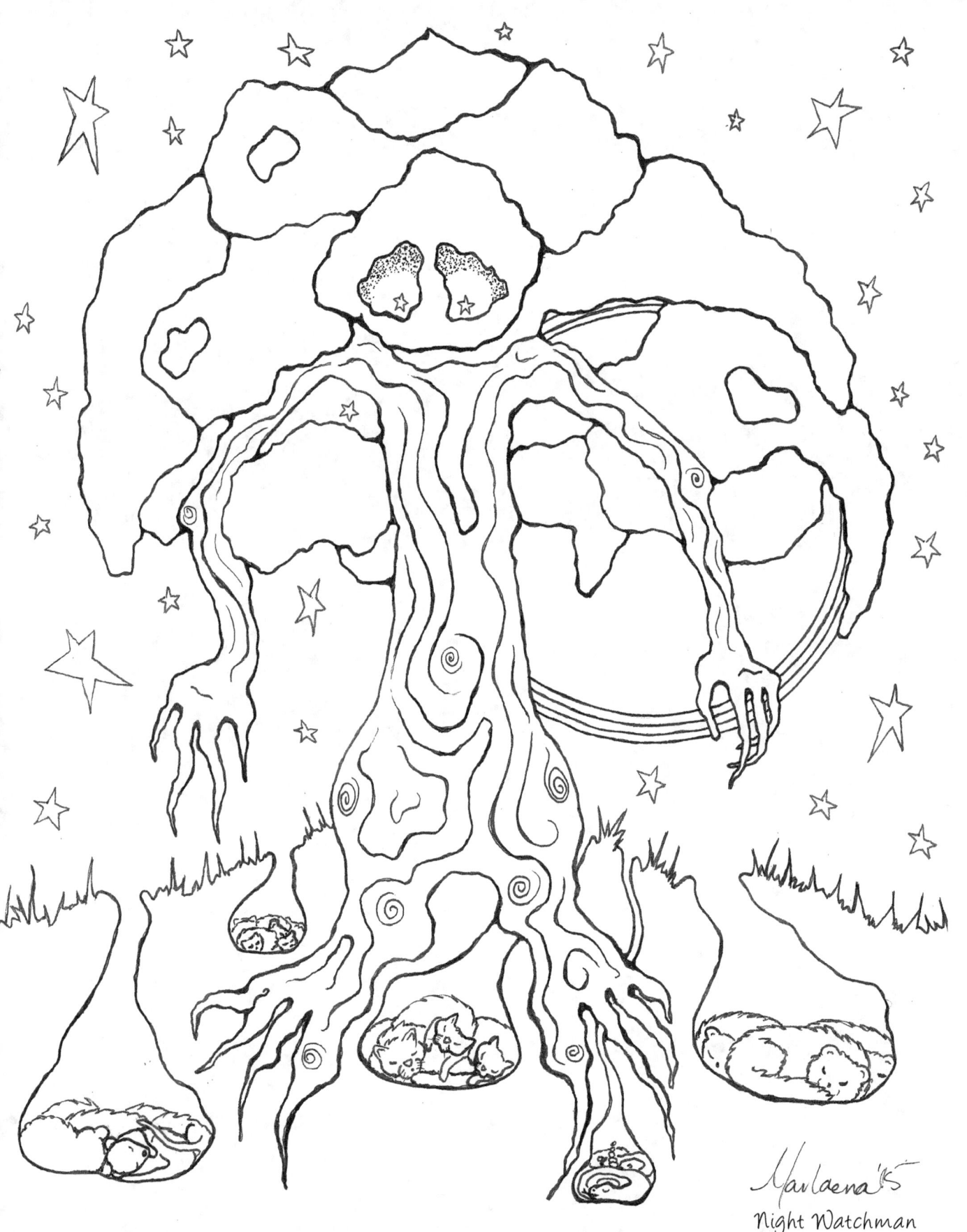

Marlaena '15

Night Watchman

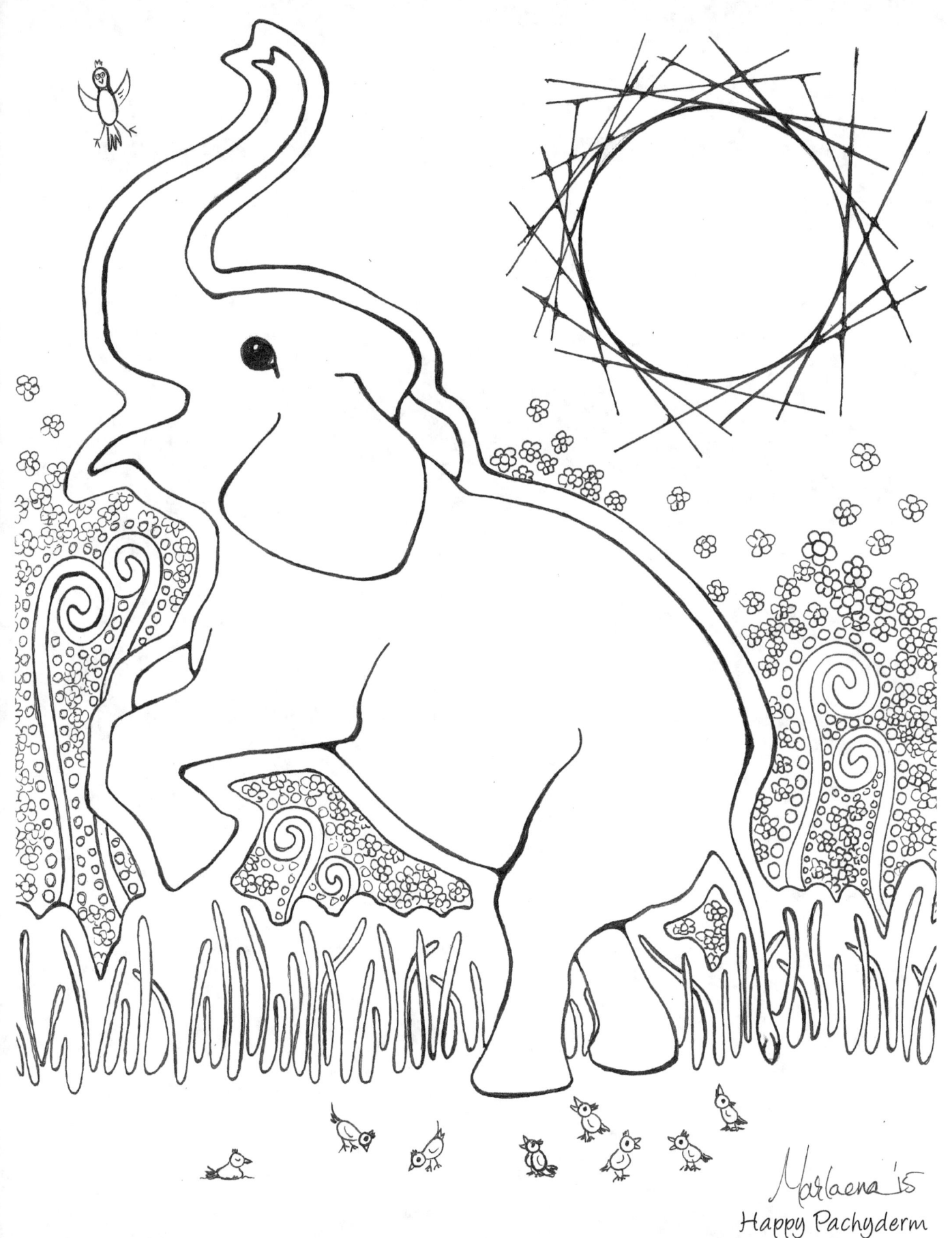

Marlaena '15

Happy Pachyderm

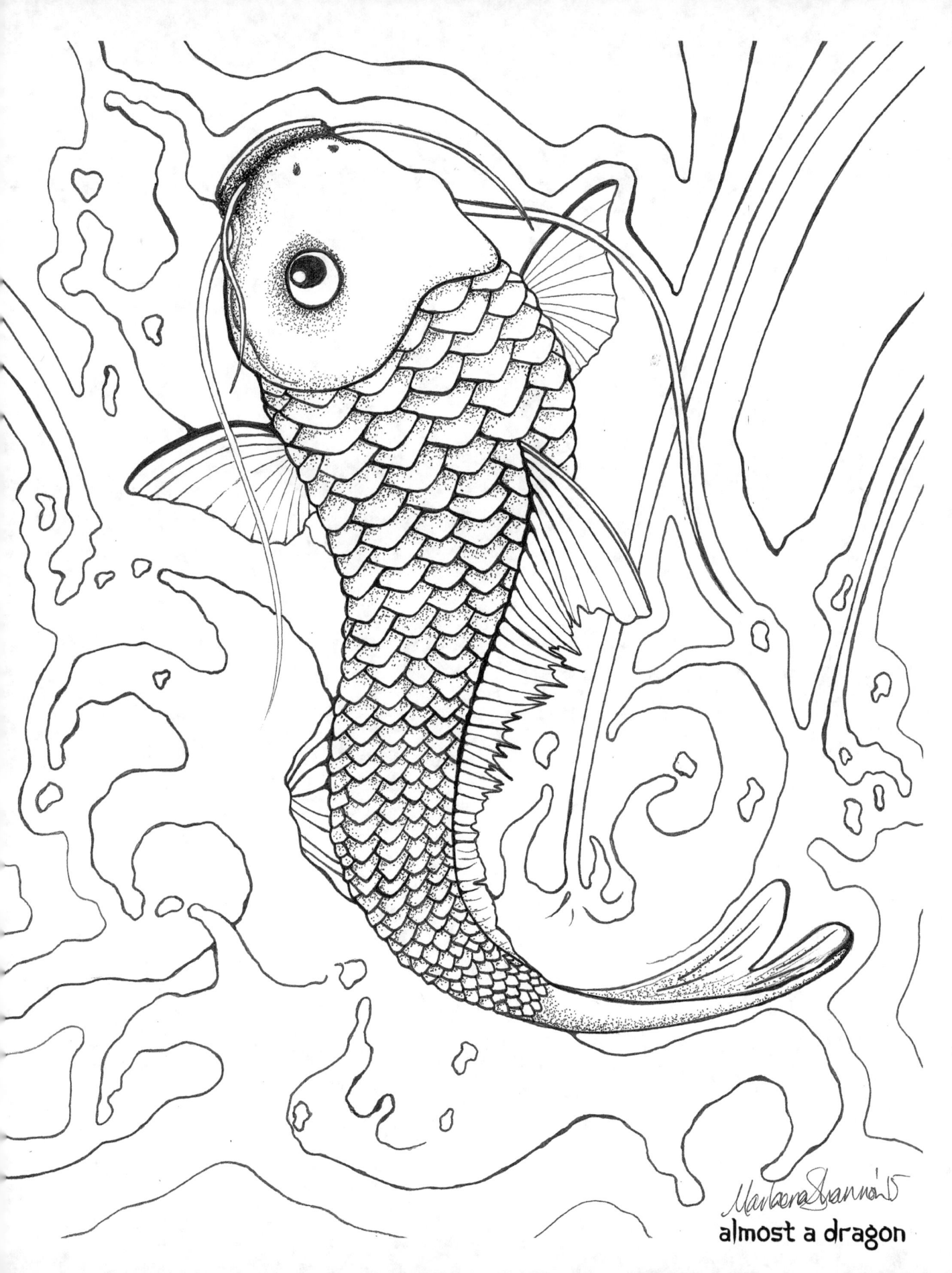

almost a dragon

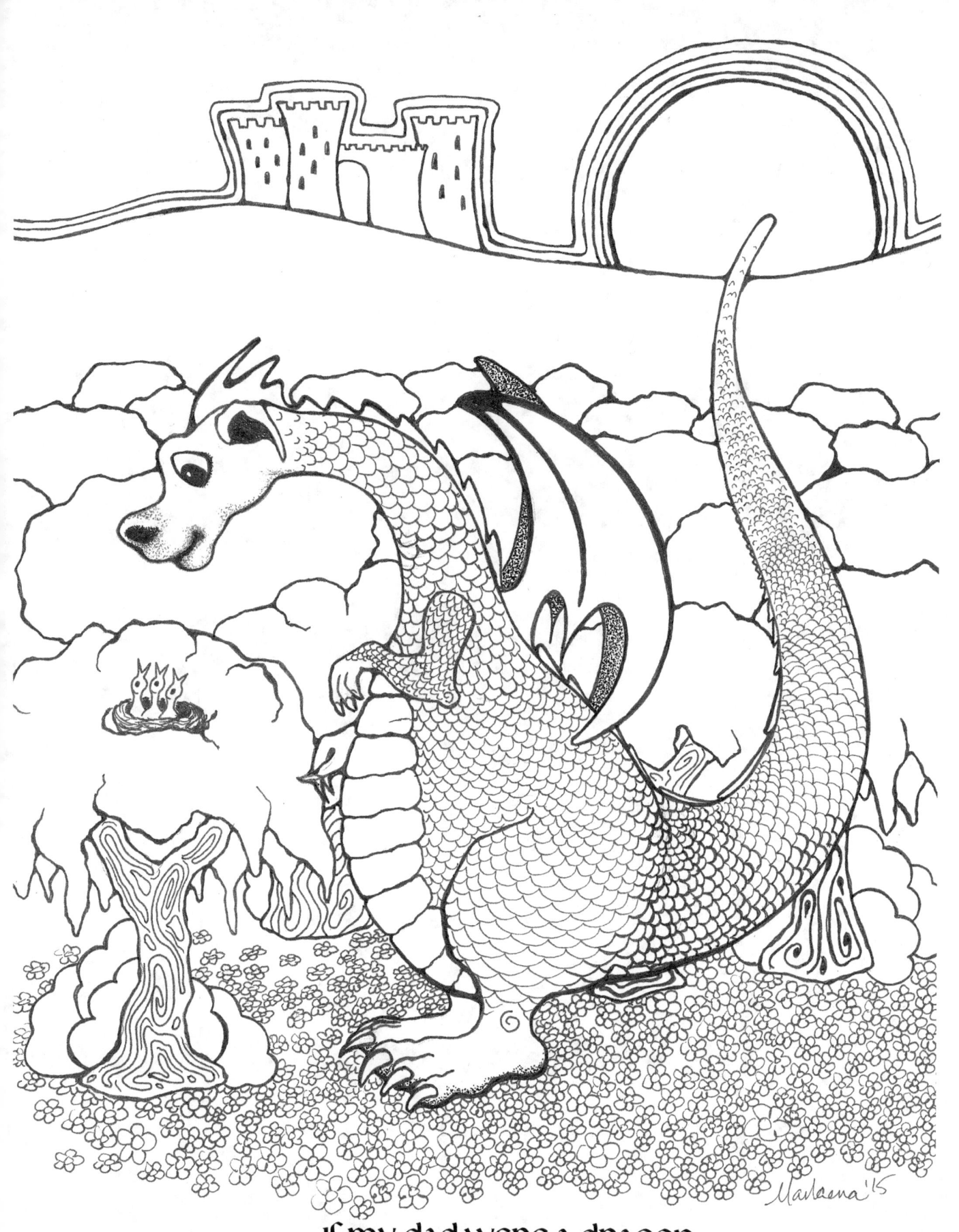

If my dad were a dragon

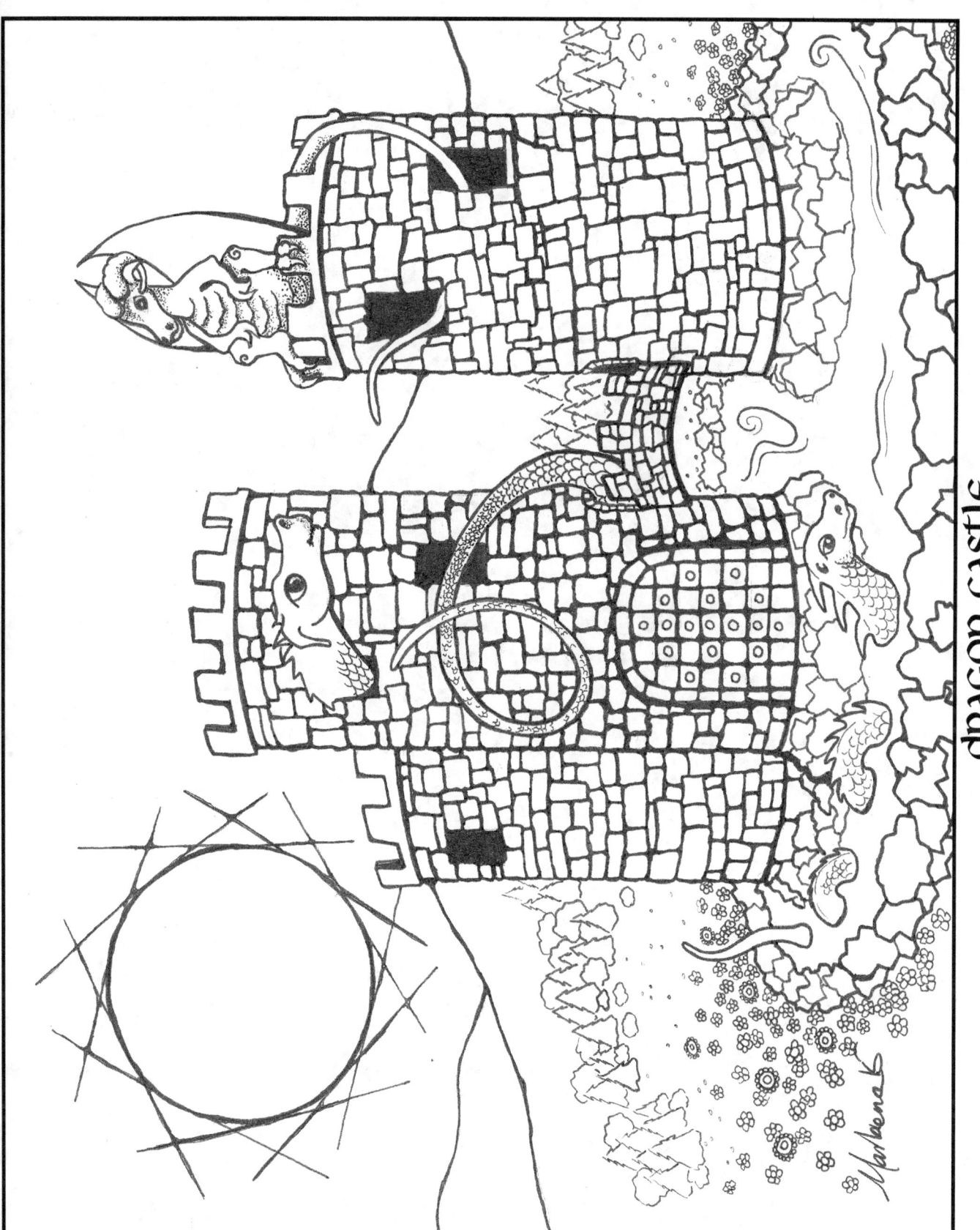

dragon castle

MOUSEBUBBLE

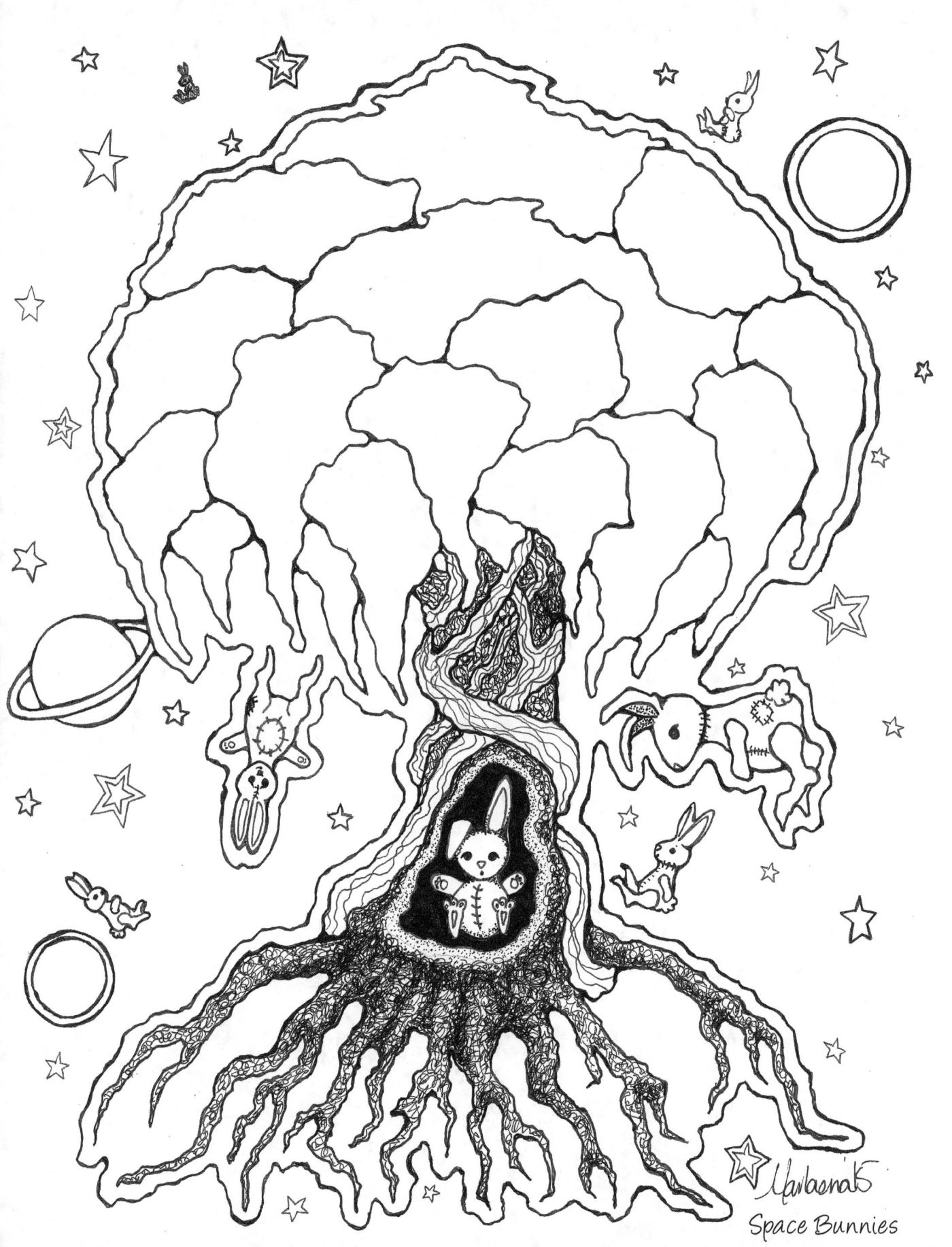

Space Bunnies

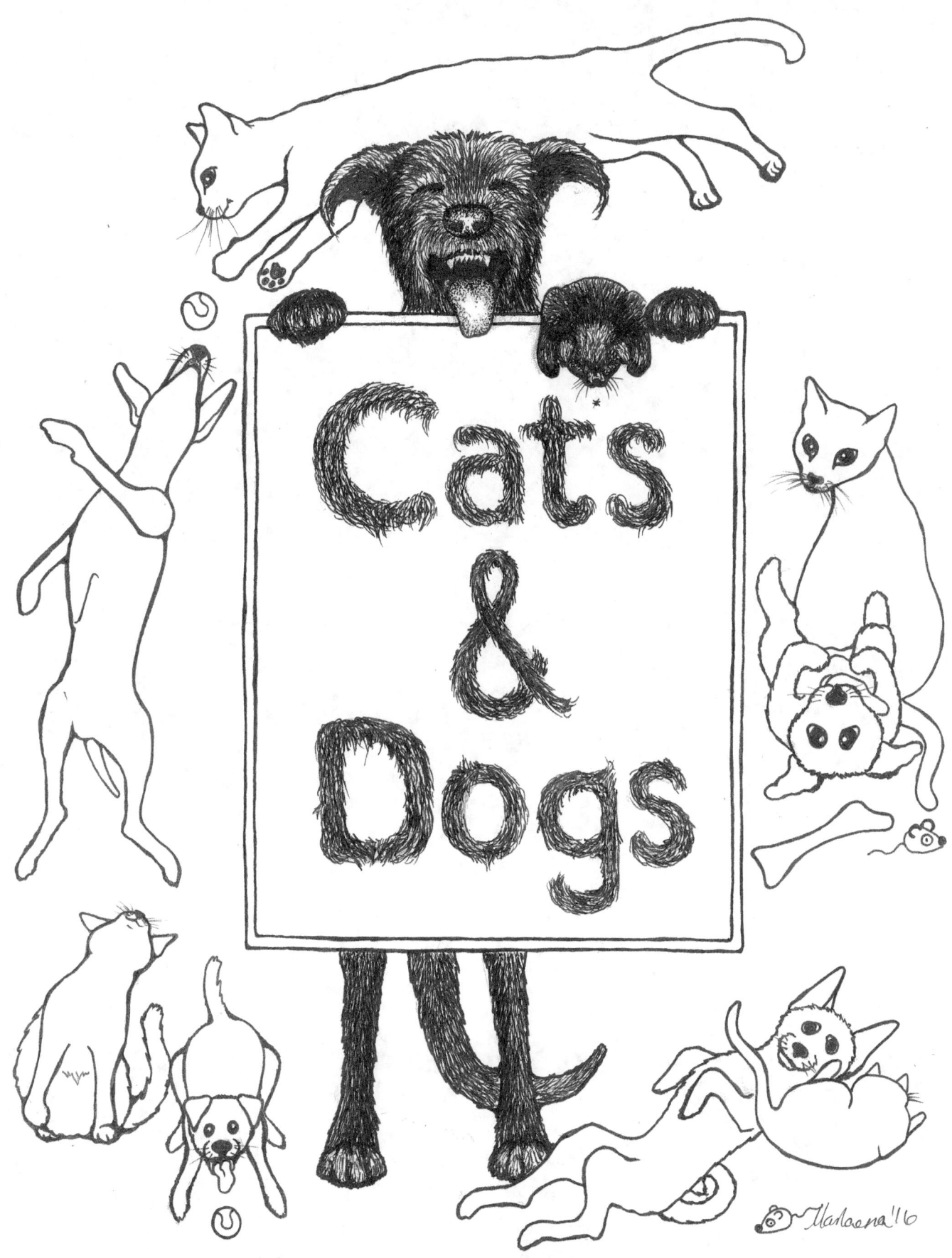

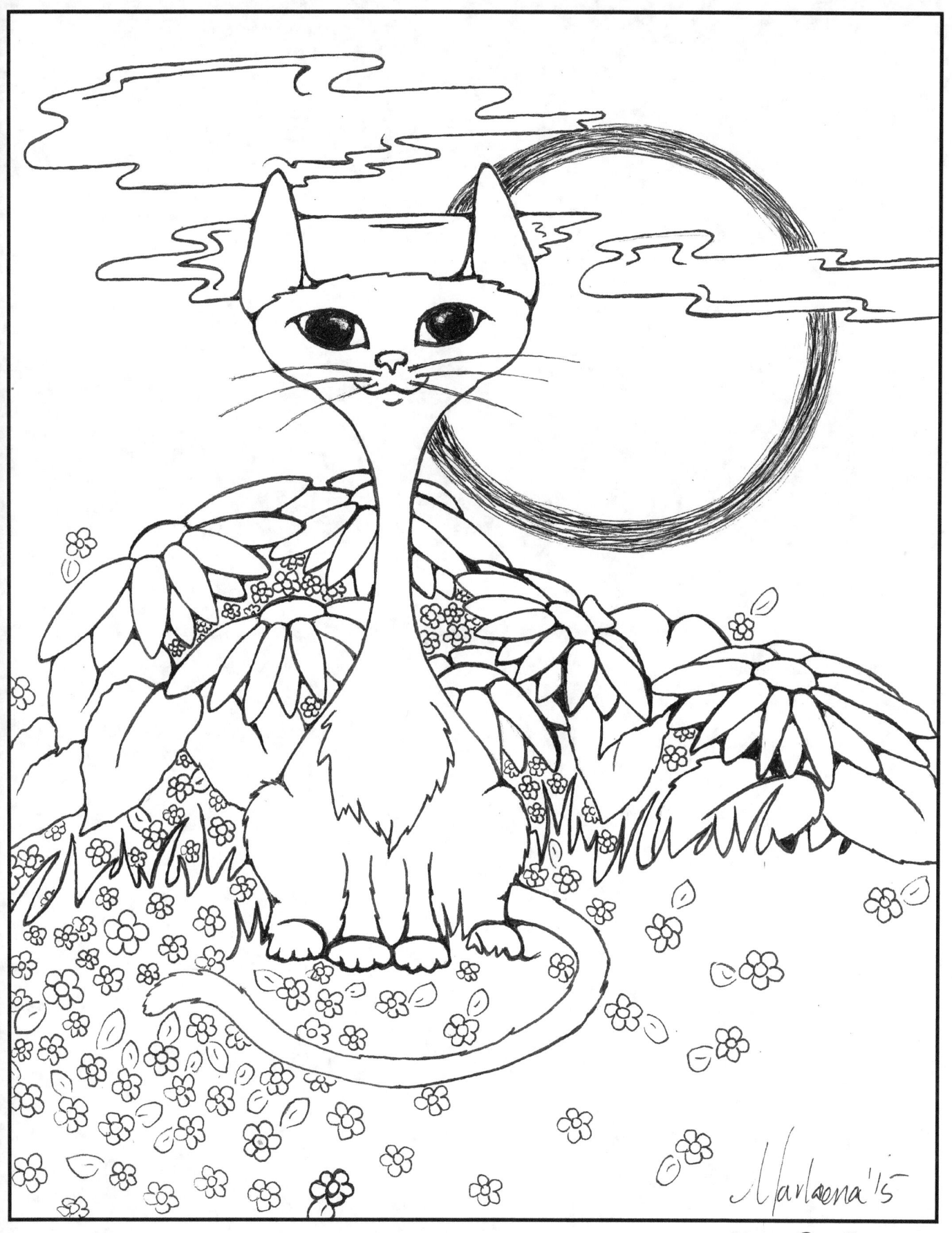

Kitty In Flowers

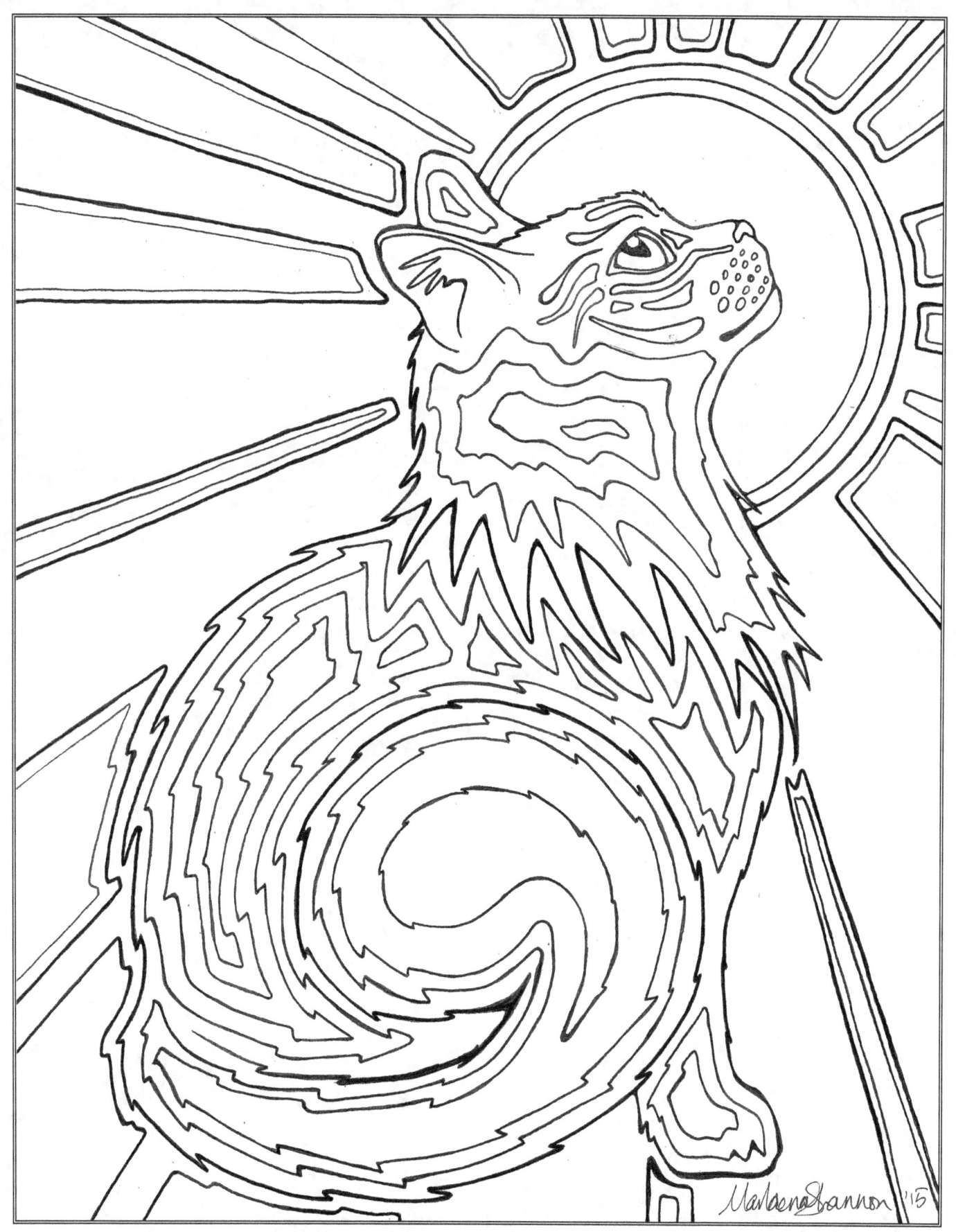

Kabrina In Heaven

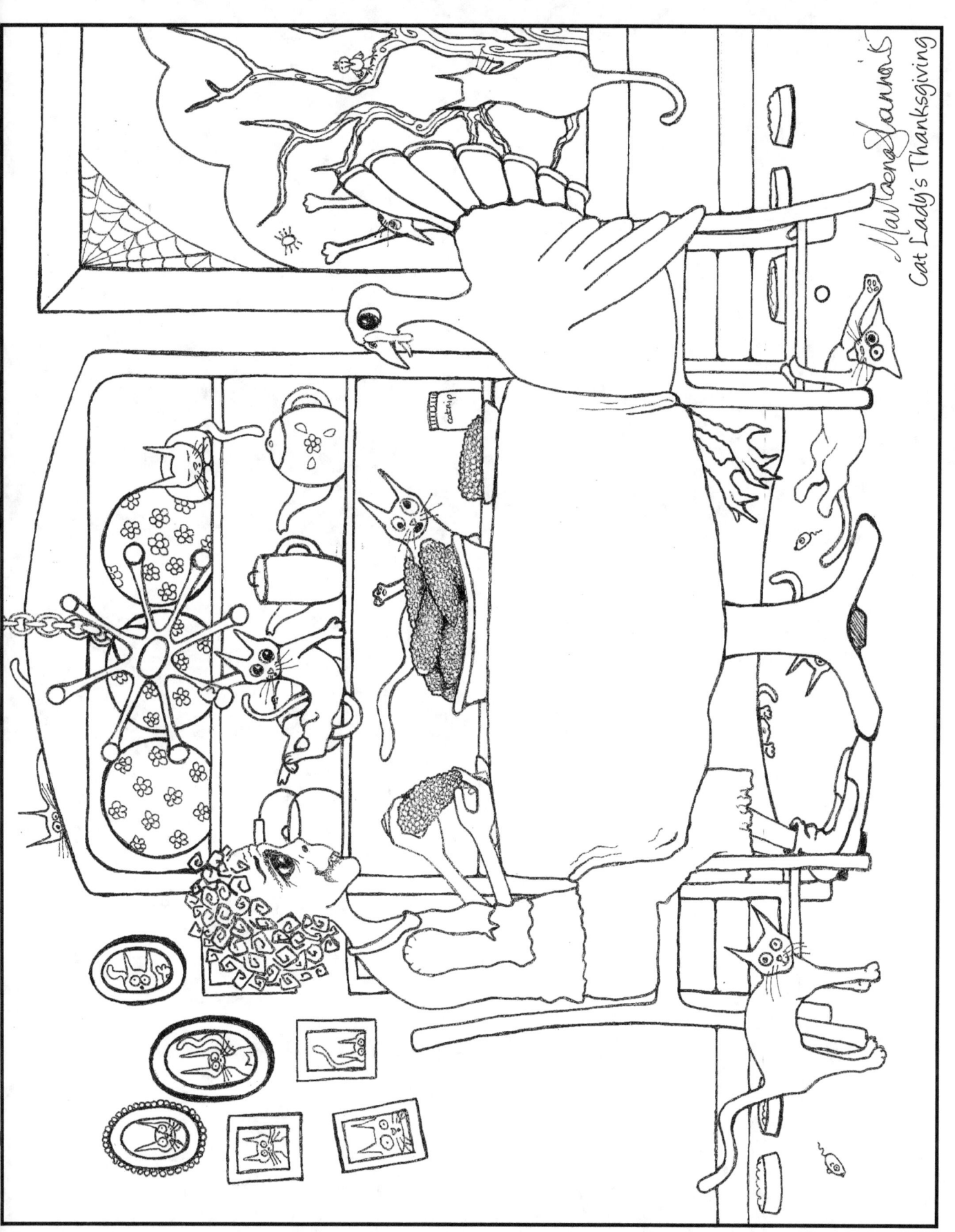

Marianne Sannon's
Cat Lady's Thanksgiving

Clowder In The Flowers

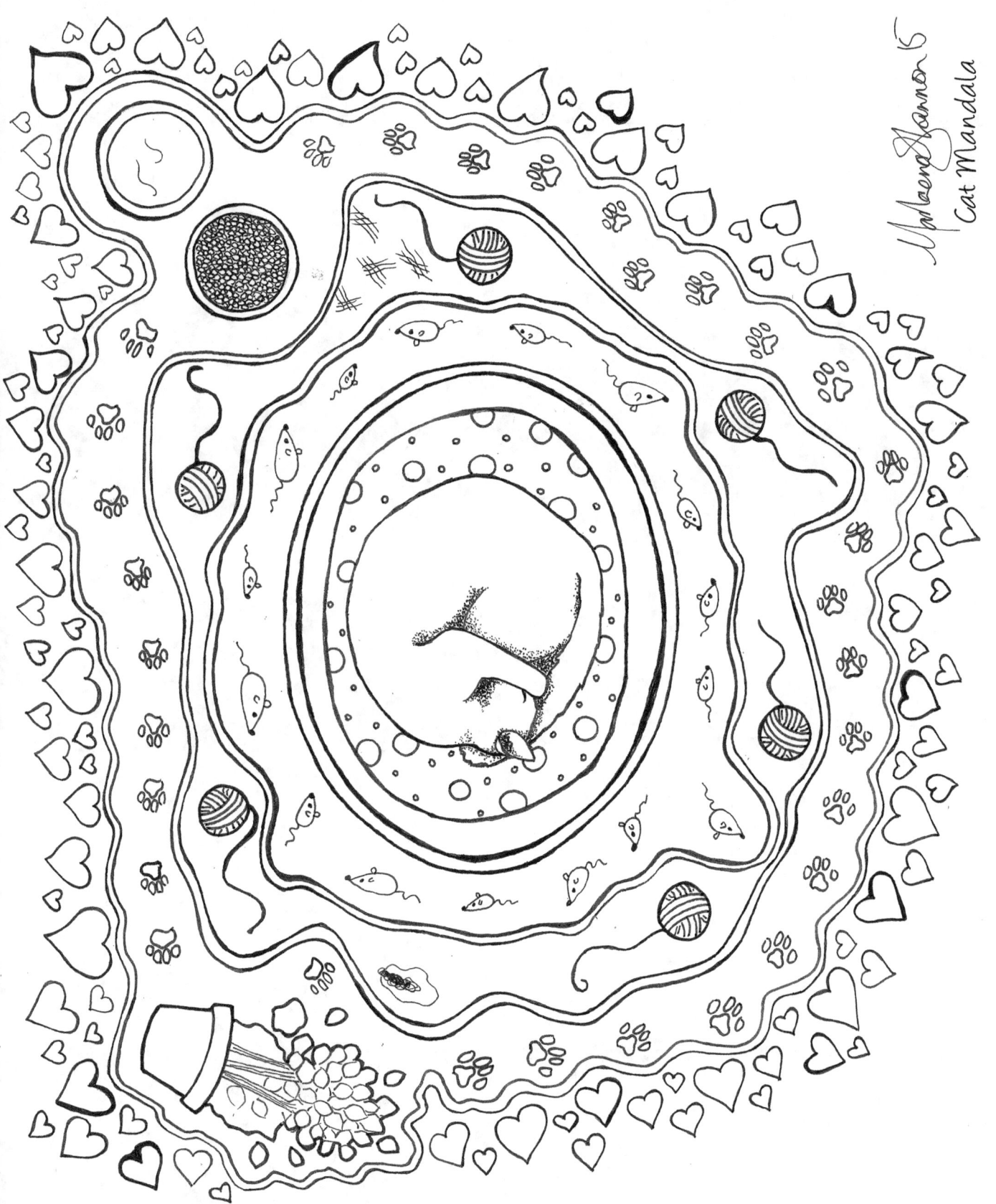

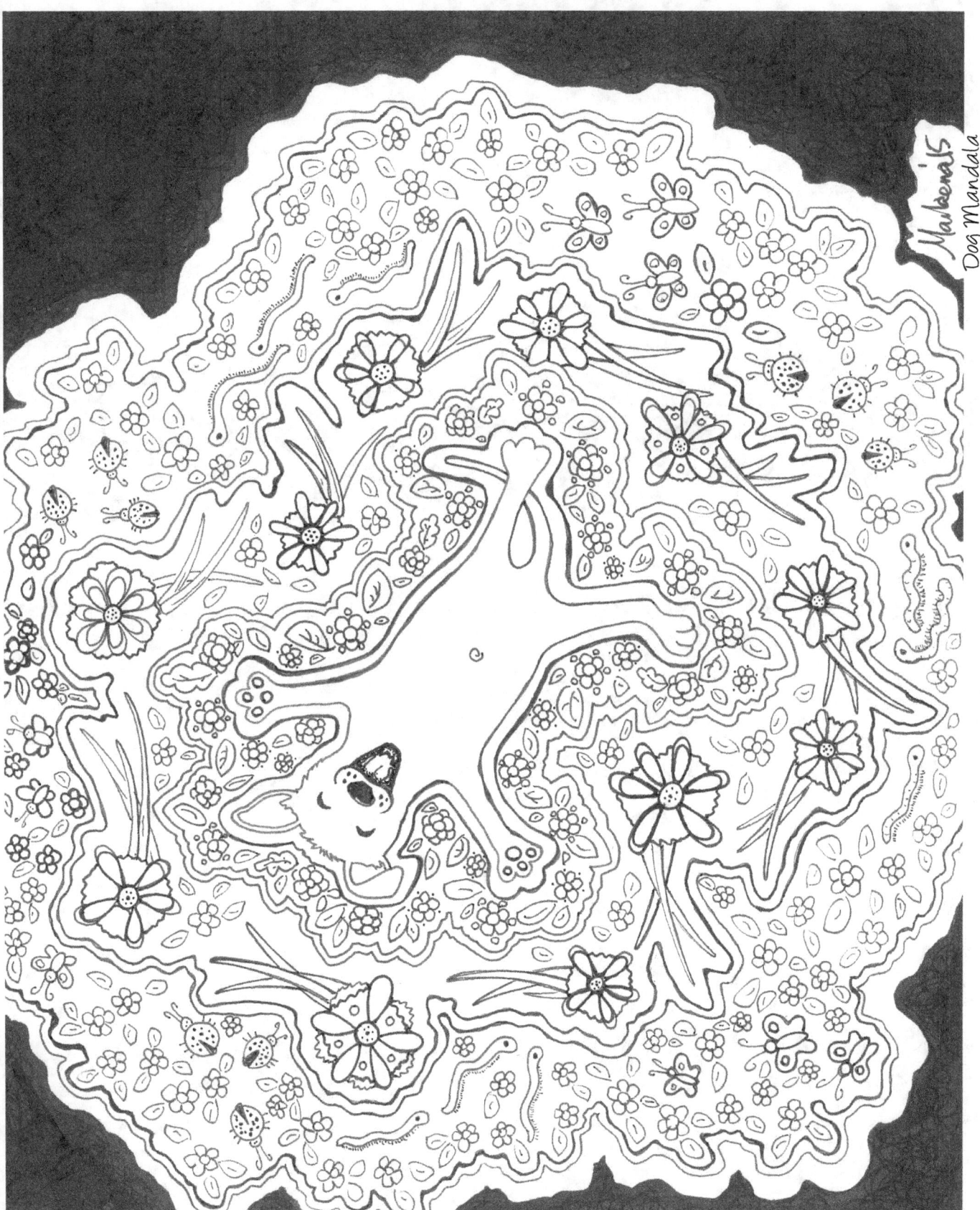

Marbeni's
Dog Mandala

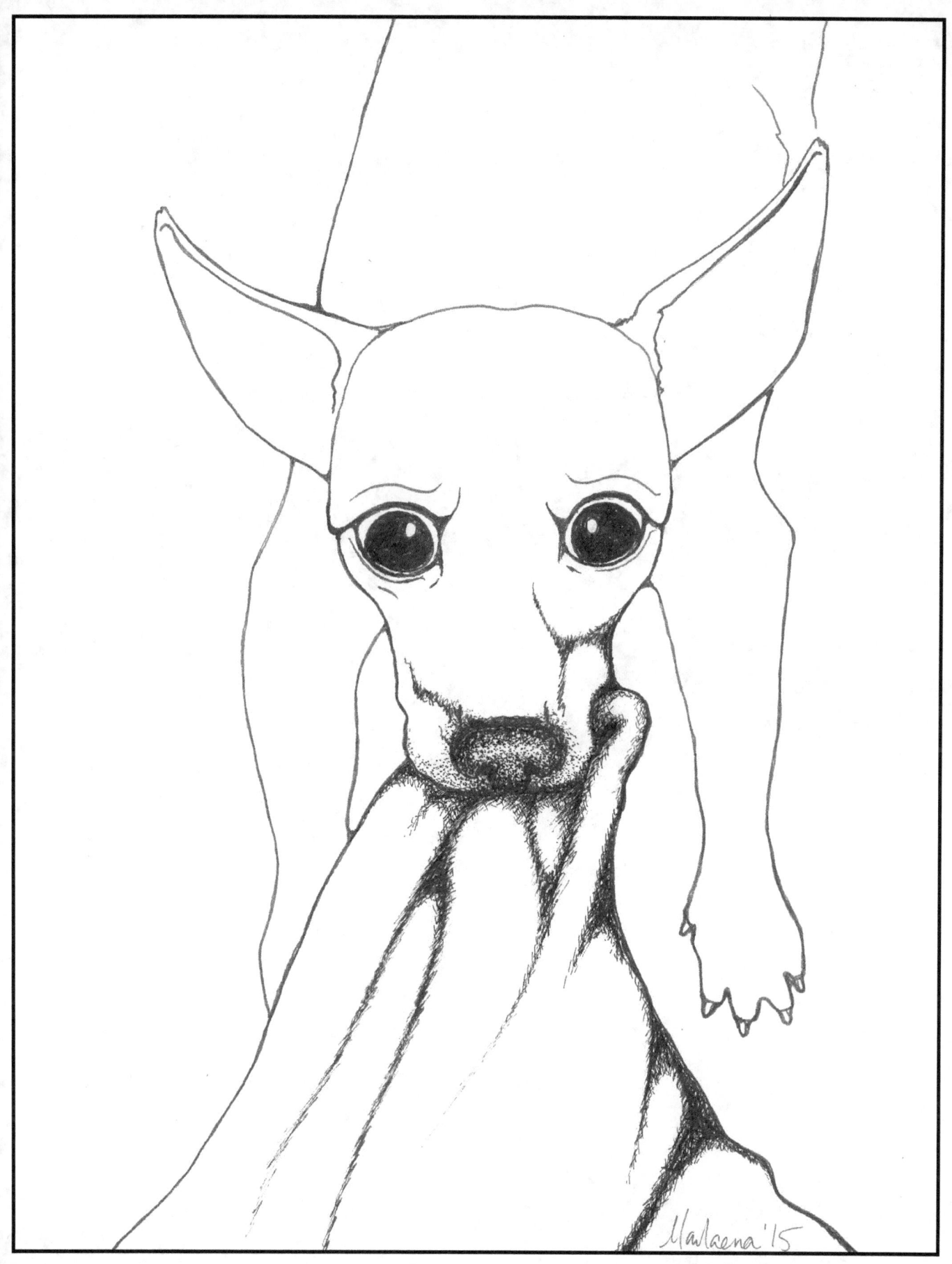

Don't Let Go

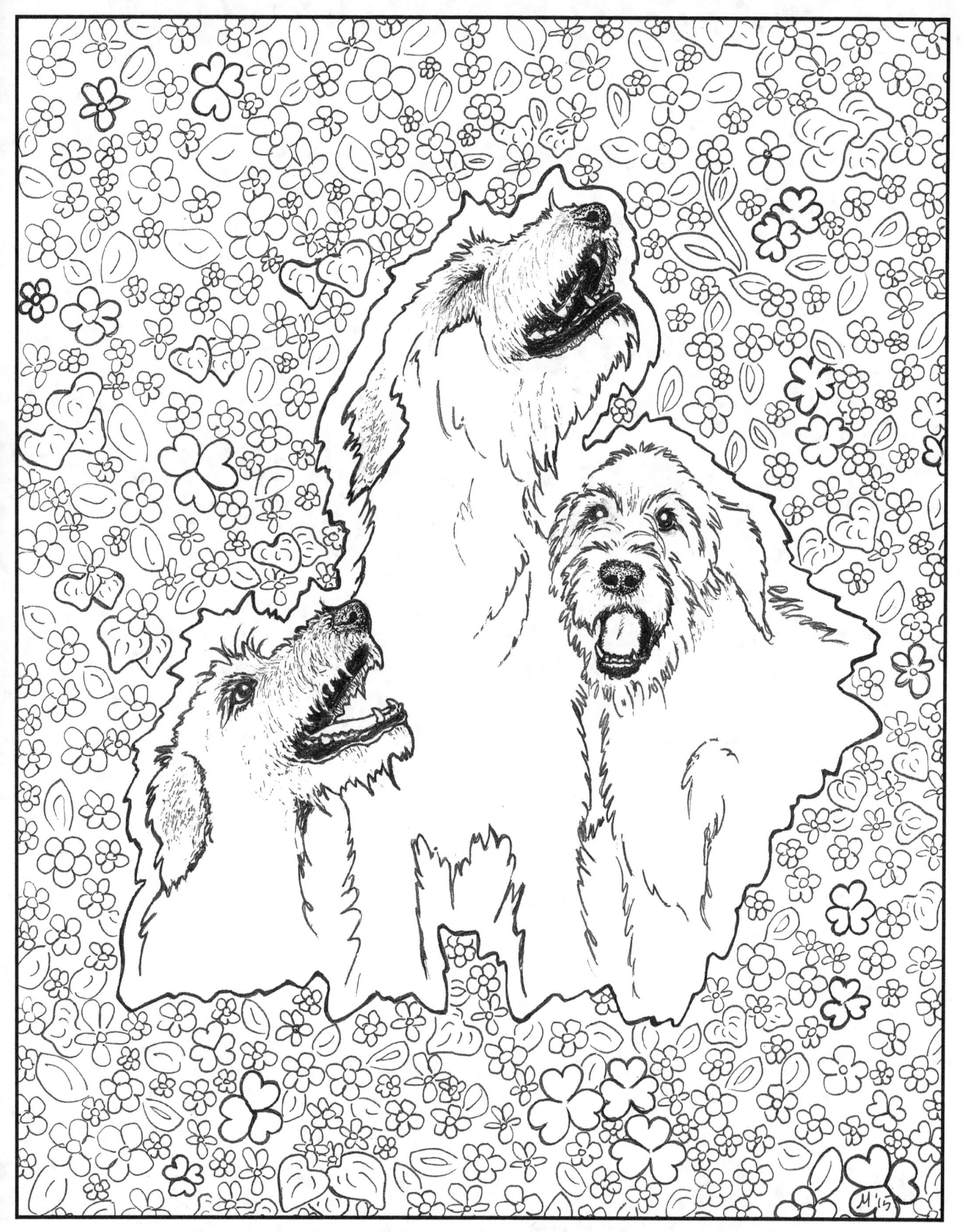

luna, maddy & kili of rohan's irish wolfhounds

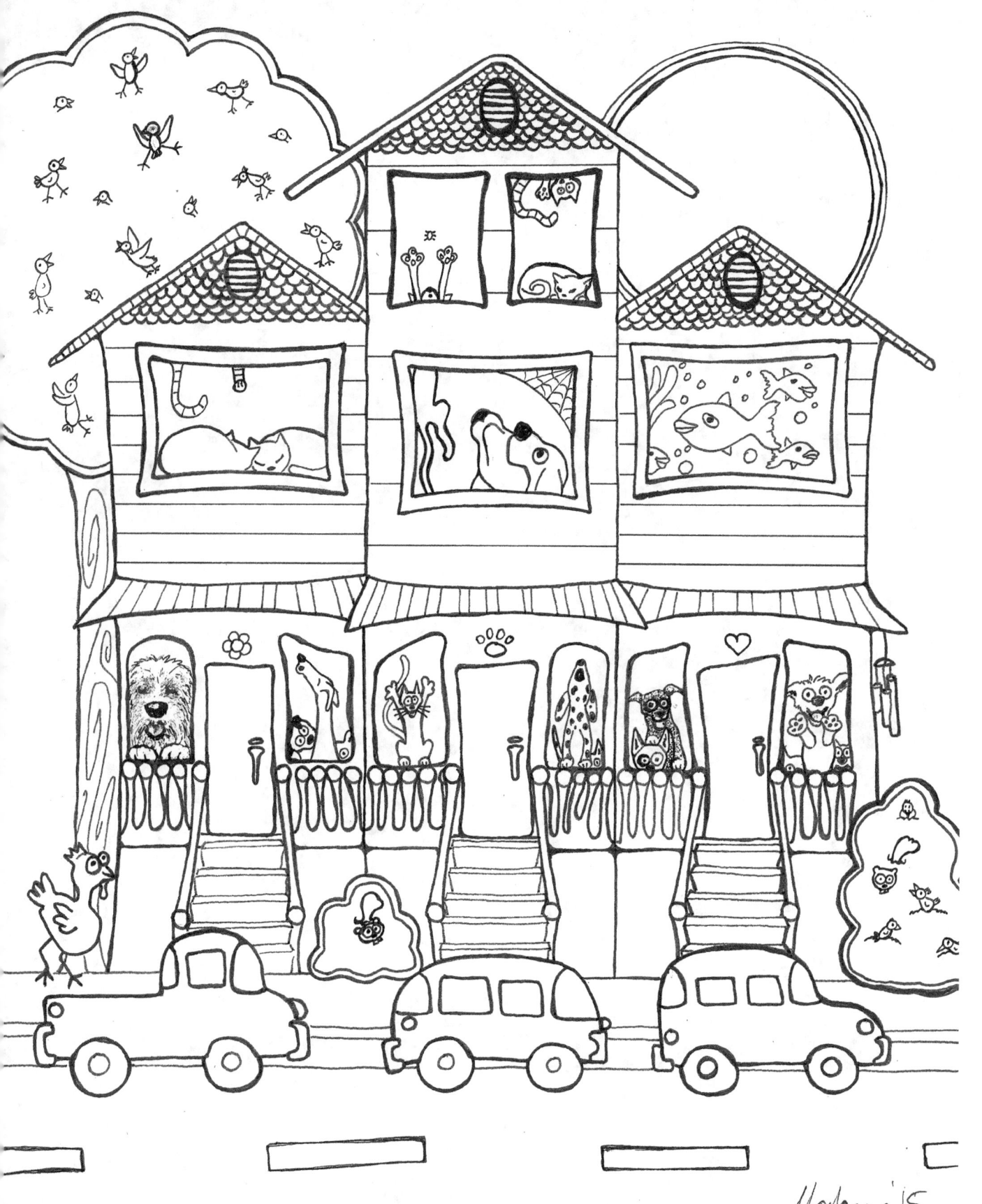

Marlaena'15
Welcome Home

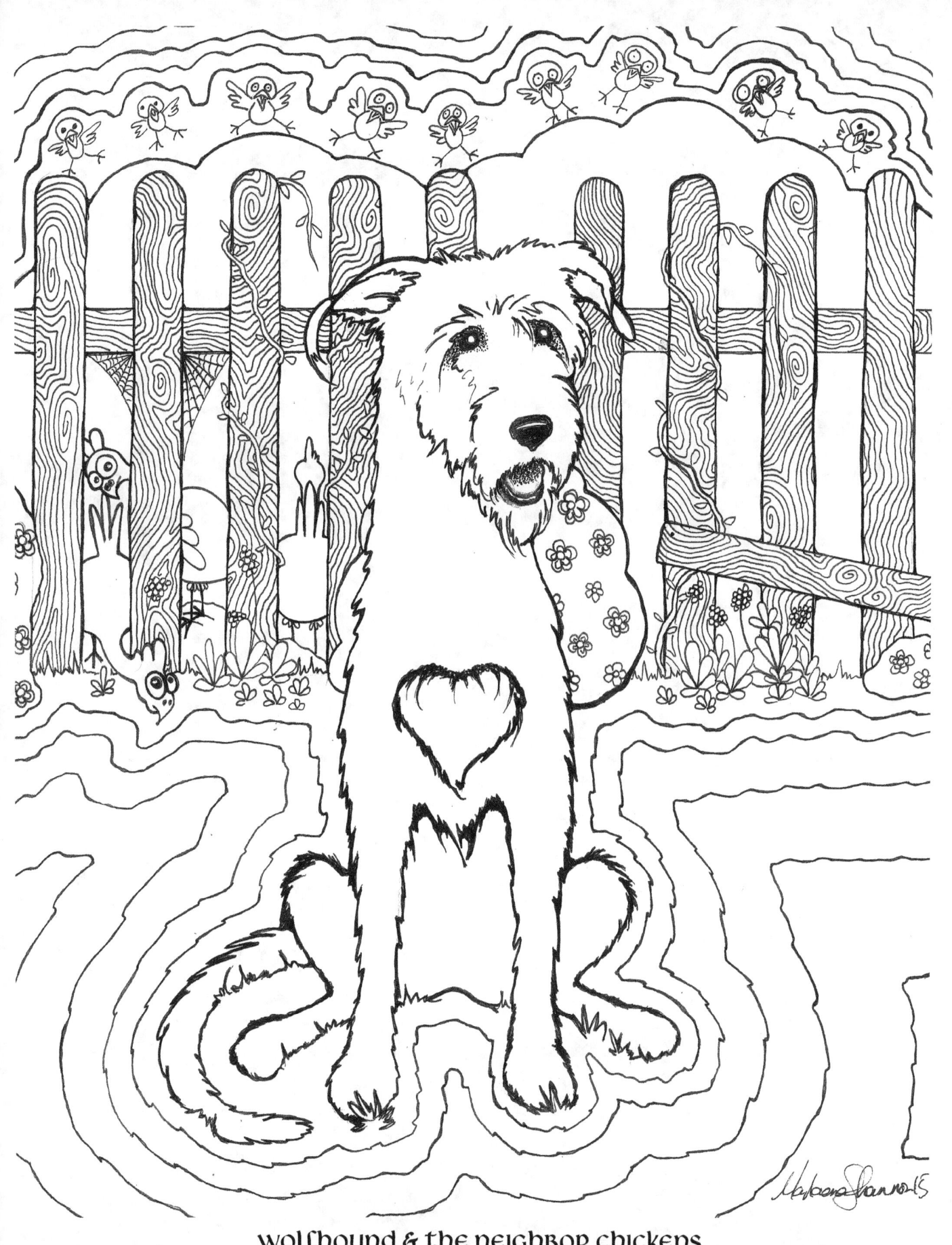

wolfhound & the neighbor chickens

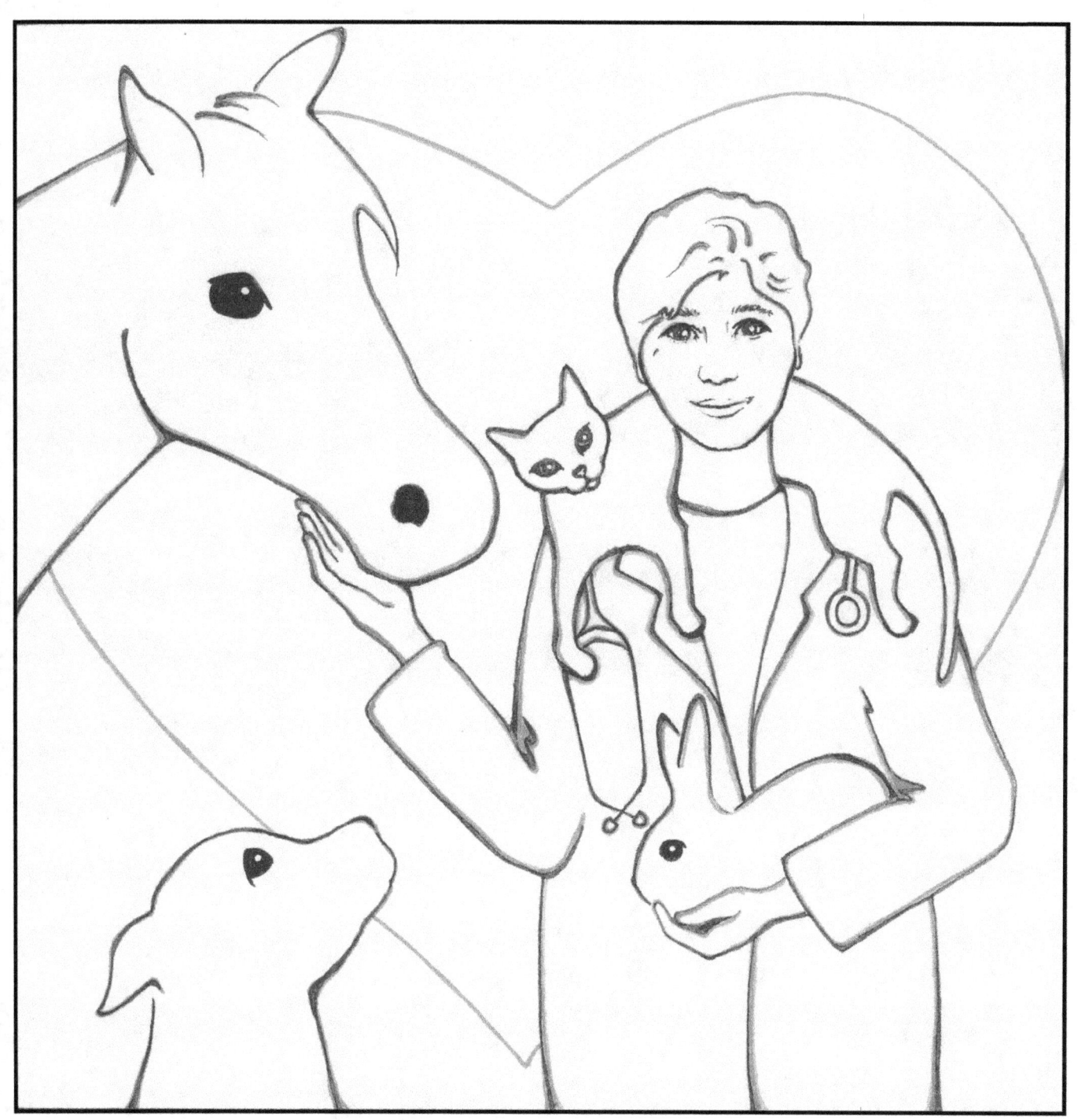

RollingHillsVeterinary.com

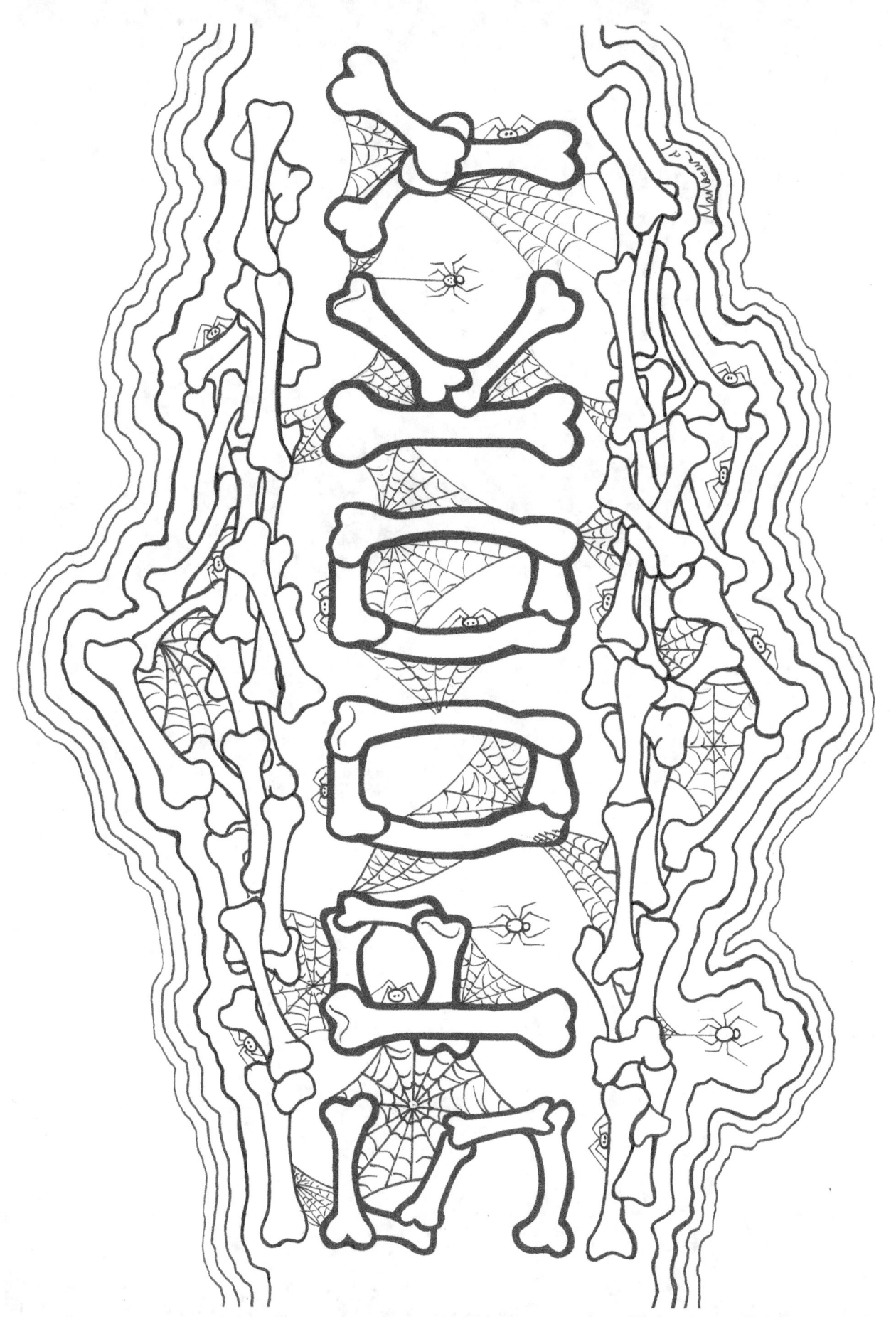

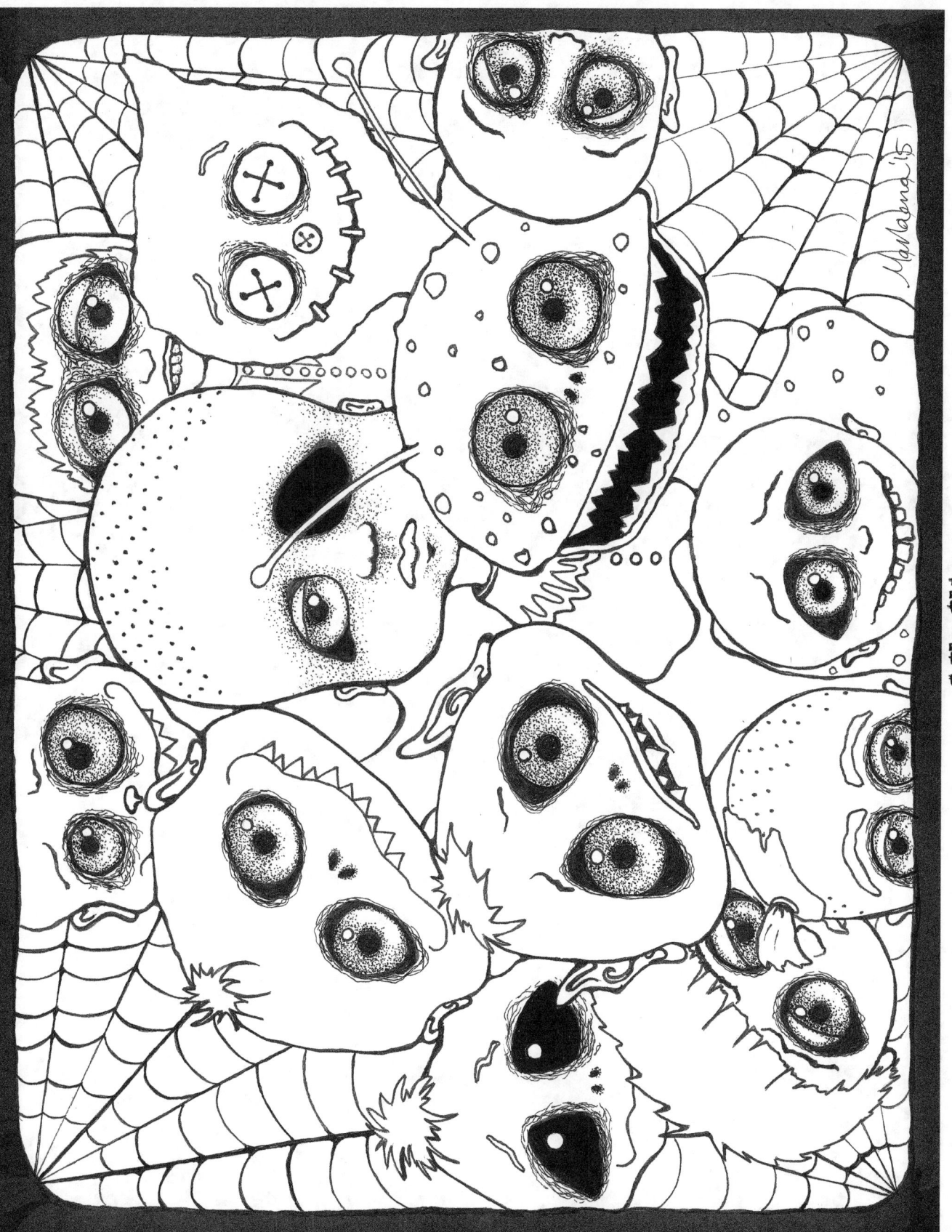

Misfits

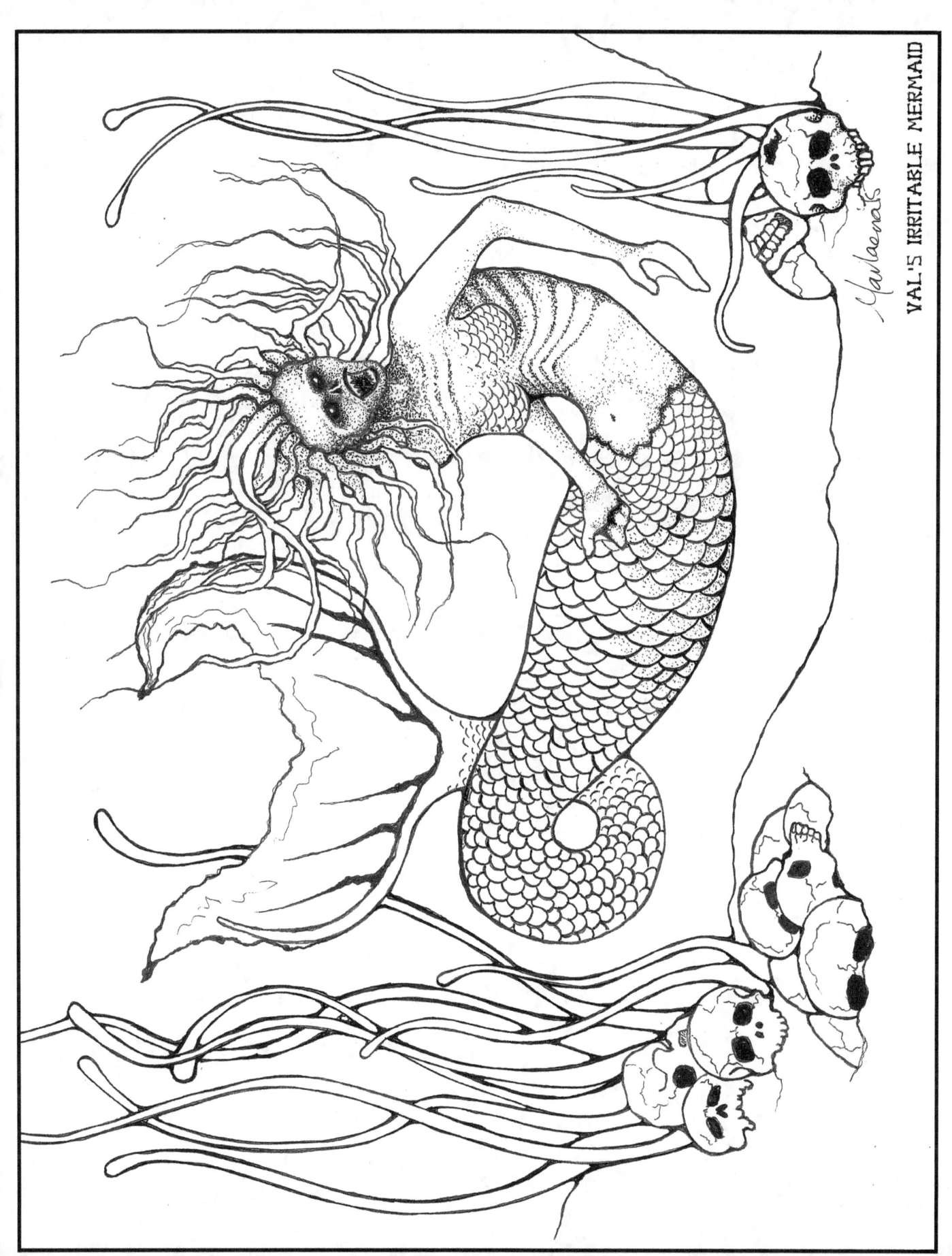

VAL'S IRRITABLE MERMAID

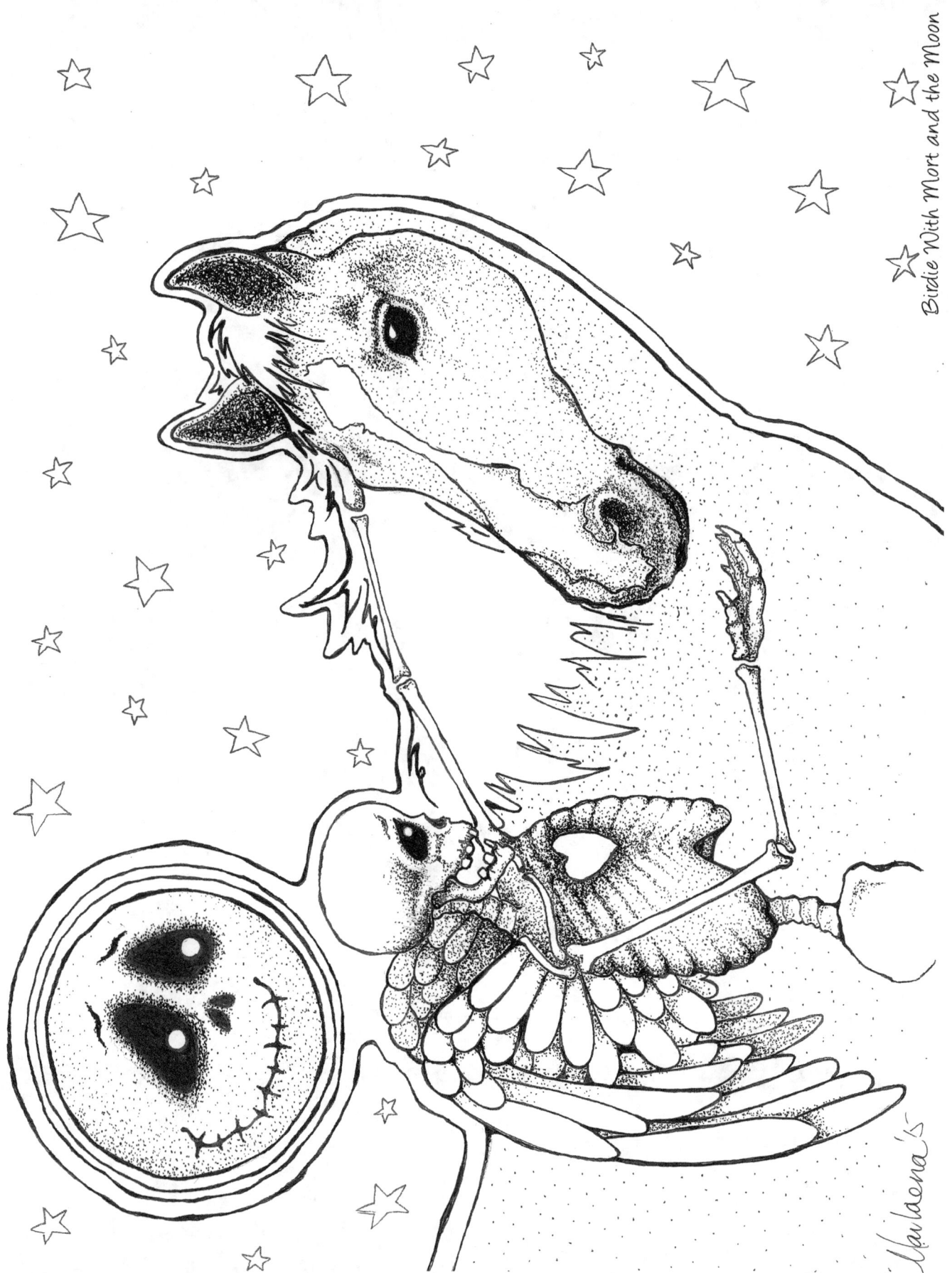

Birdie With Mort and the Moon

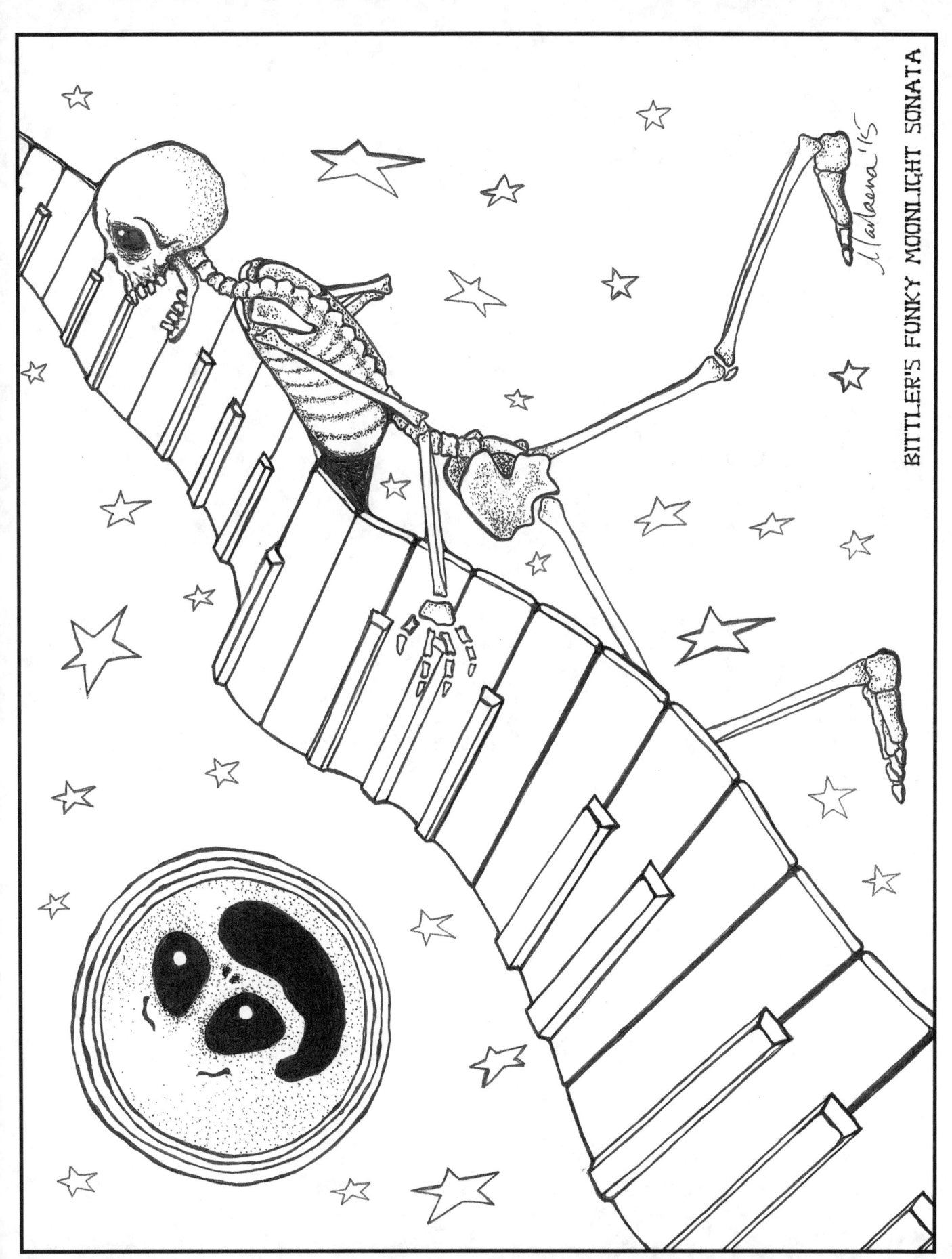

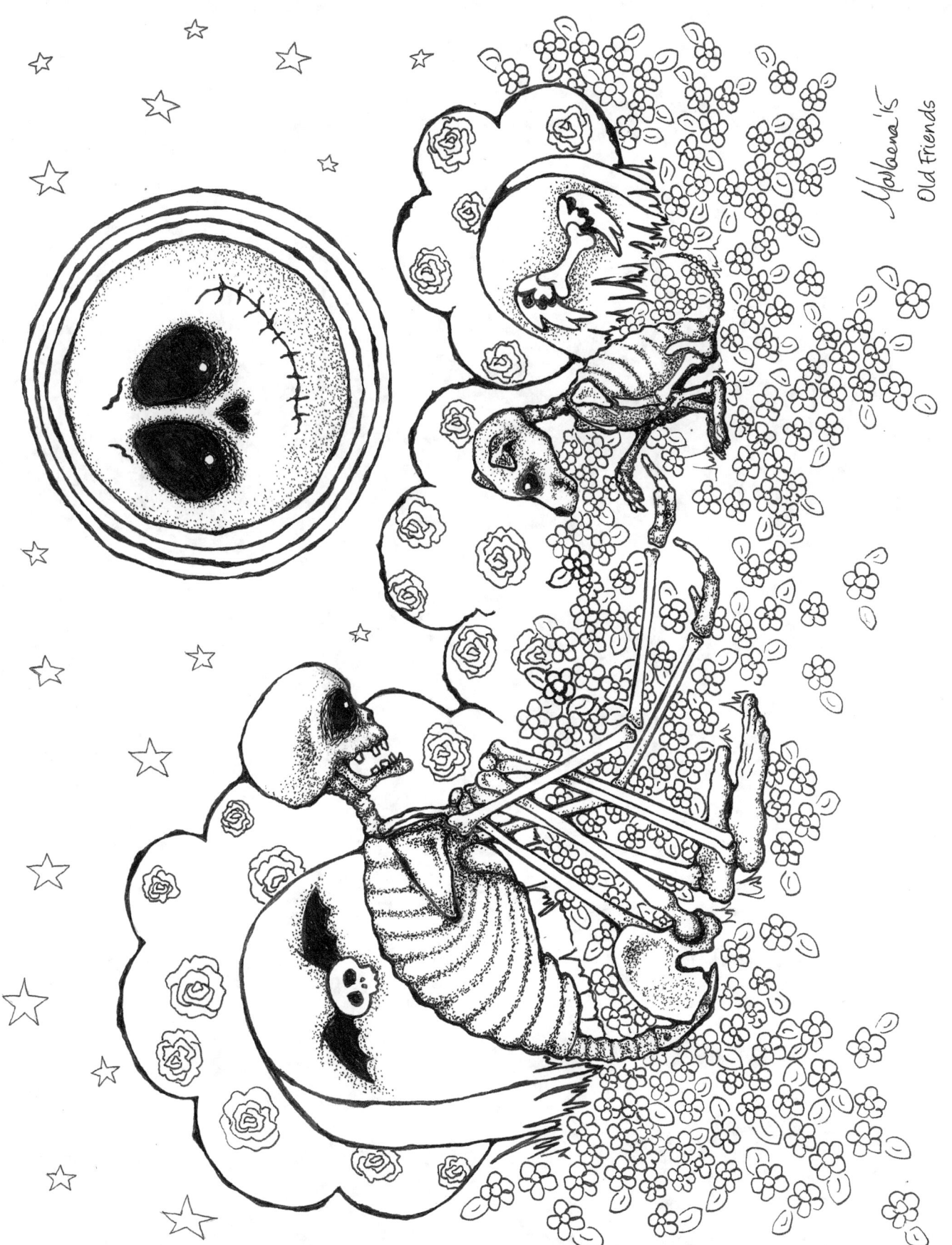

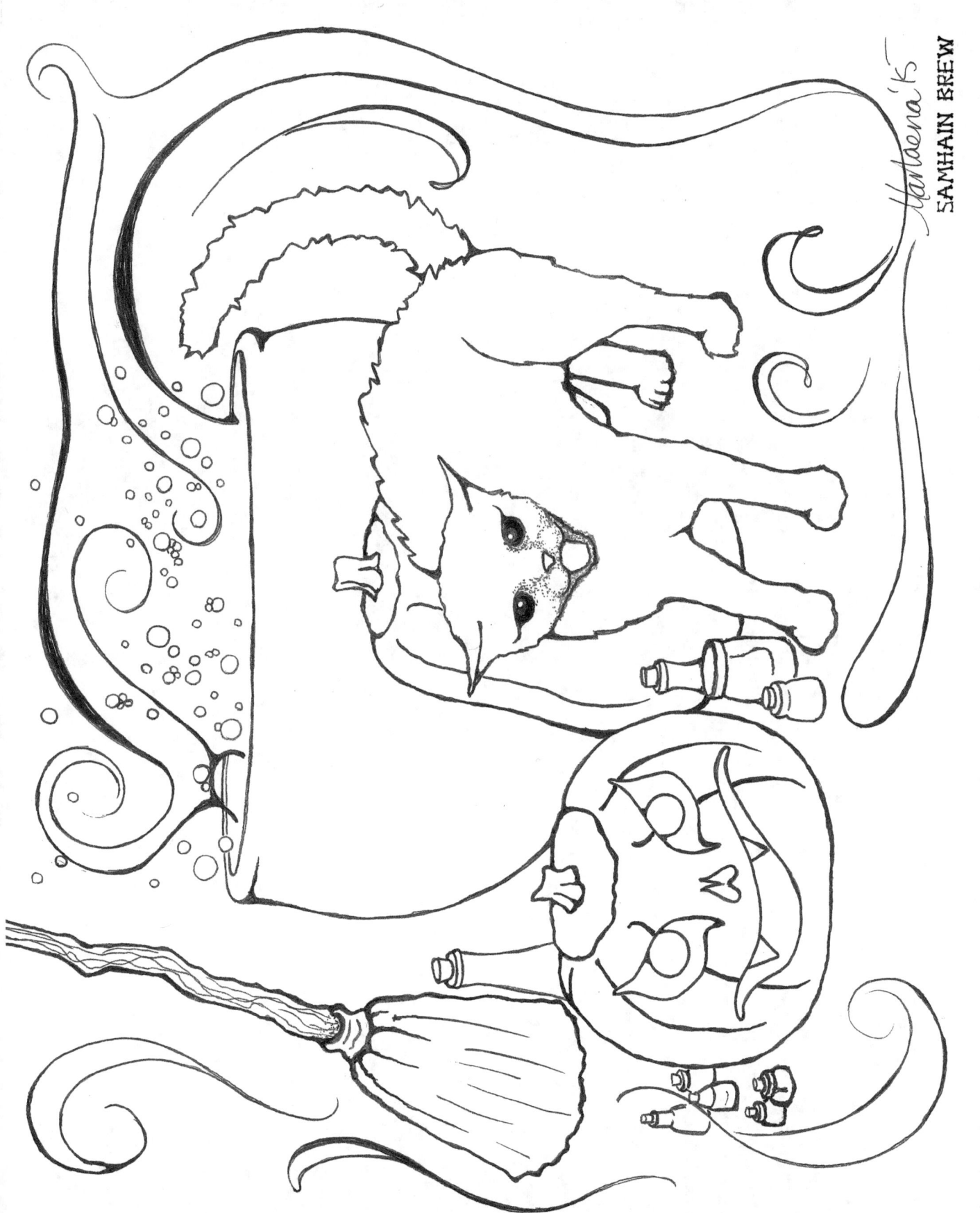

MUERTO ANGEL

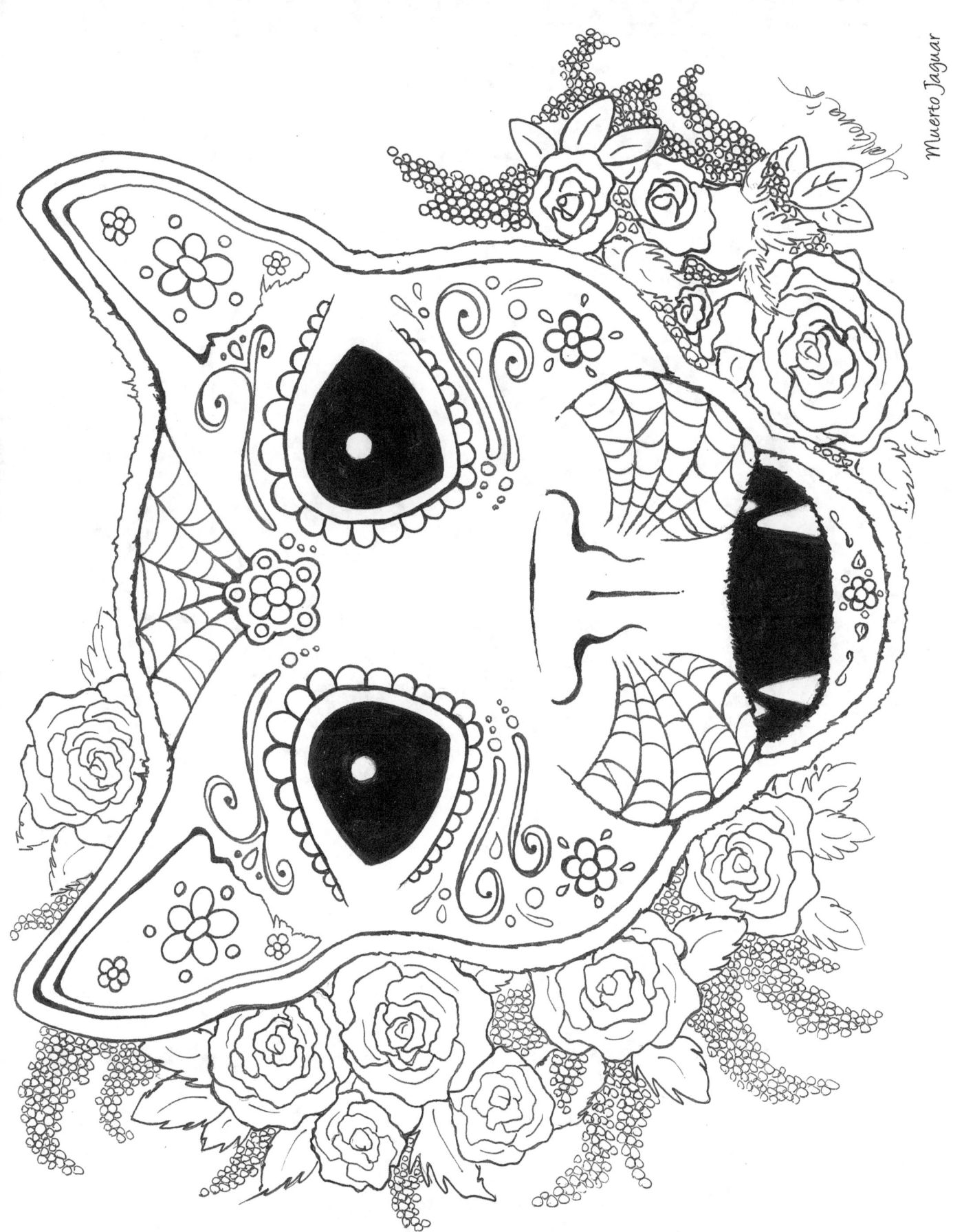

Muerto Jaguar

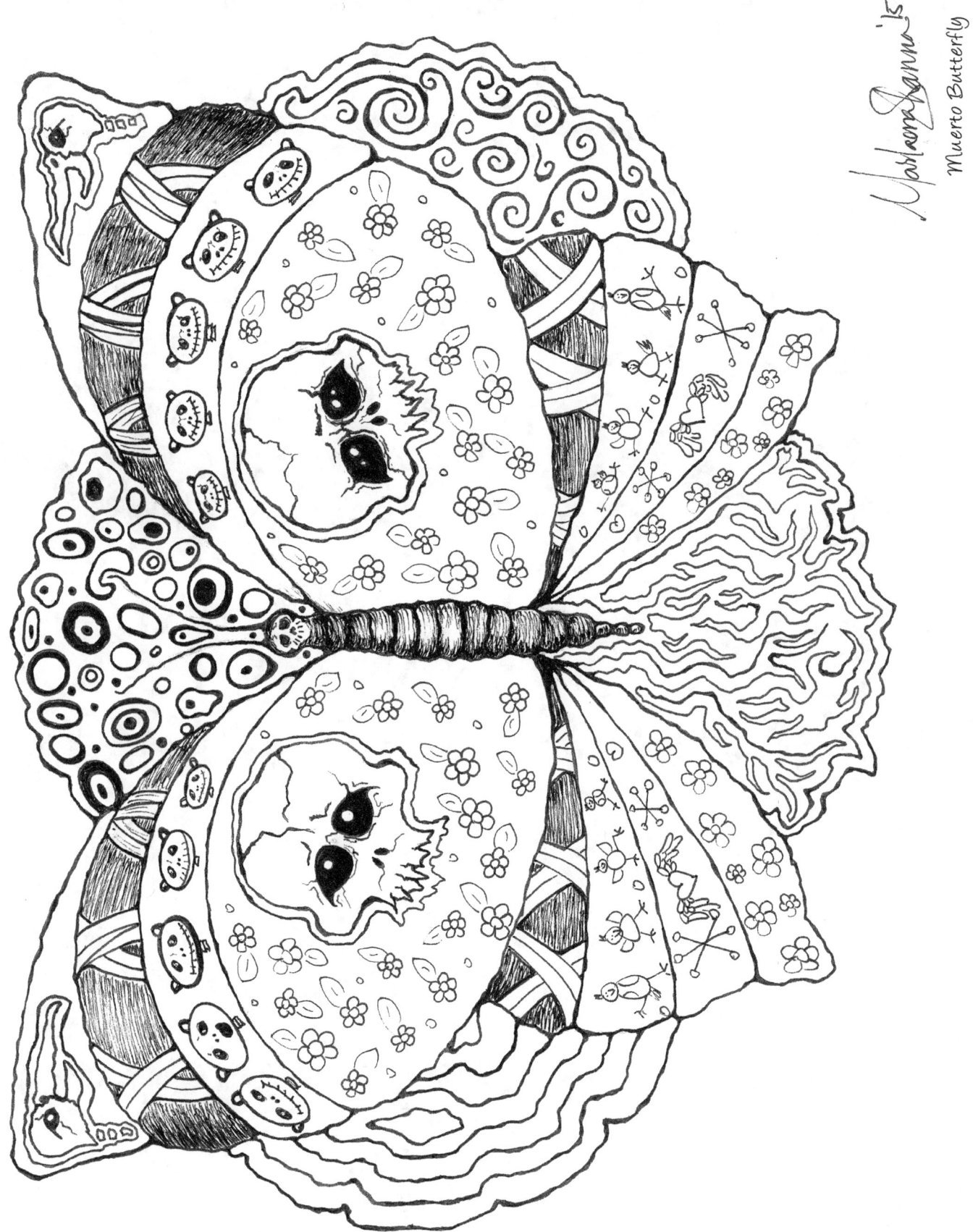

Muerto Butterfly

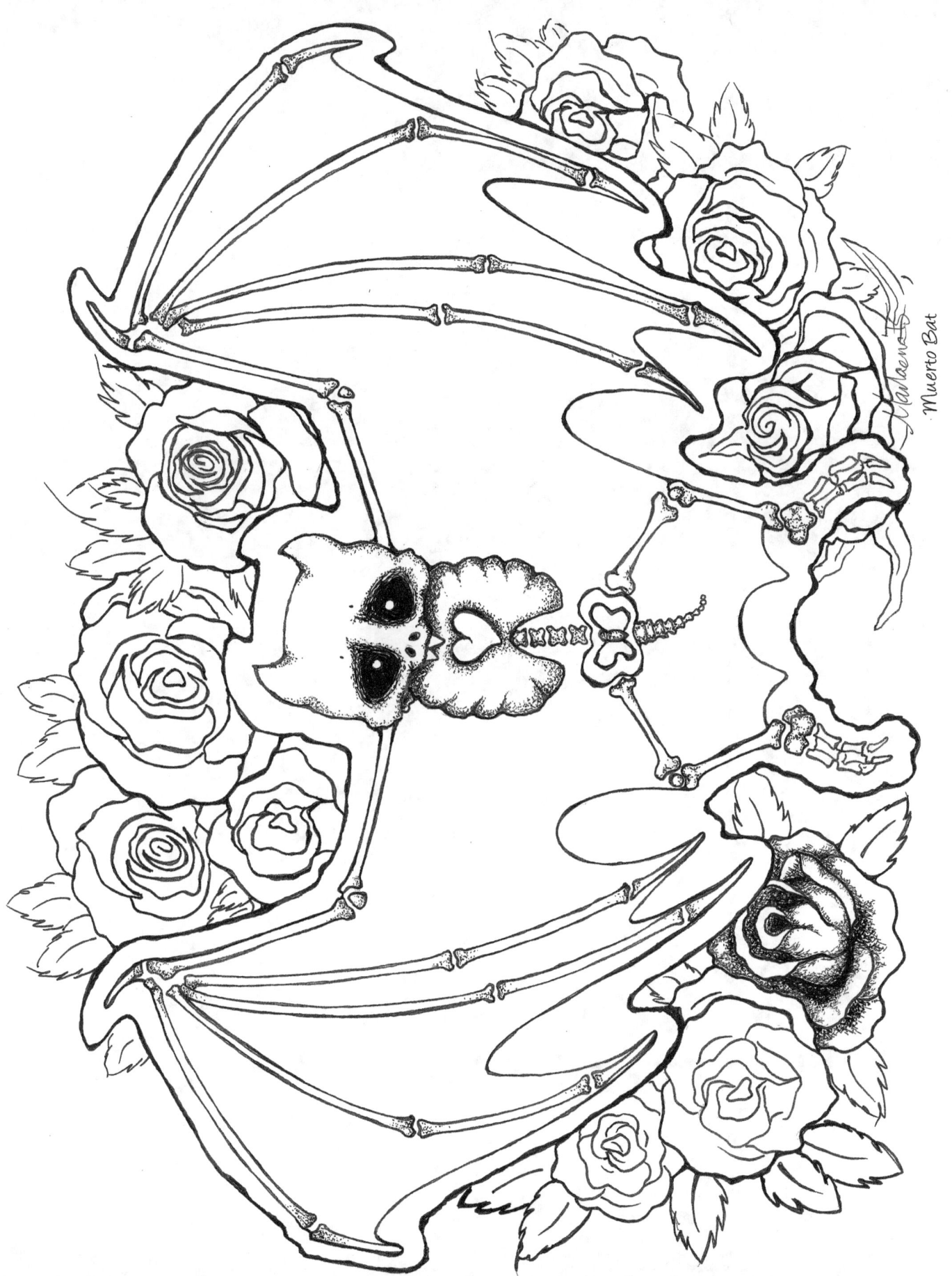

Muerto Bat

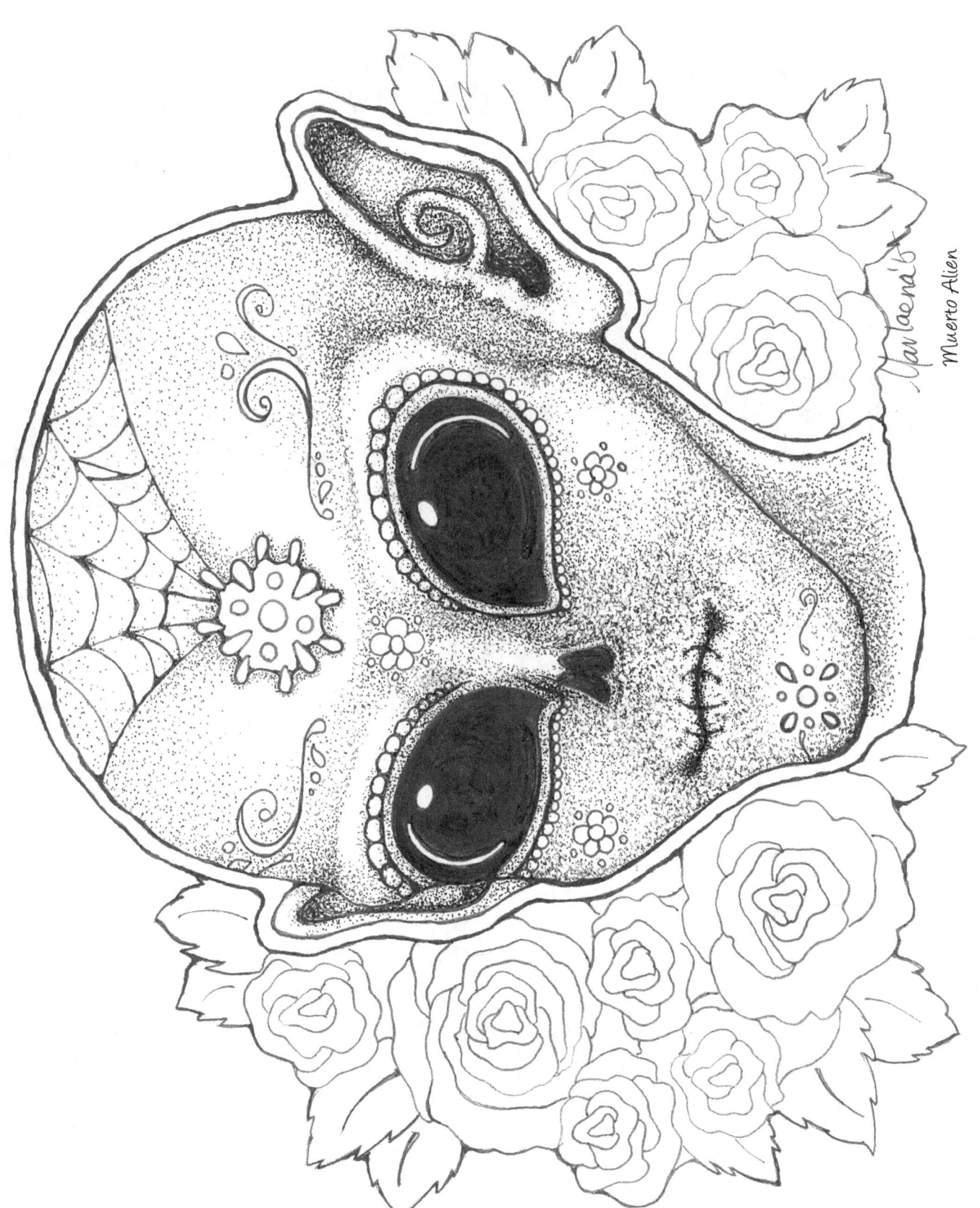

Muerto Alien

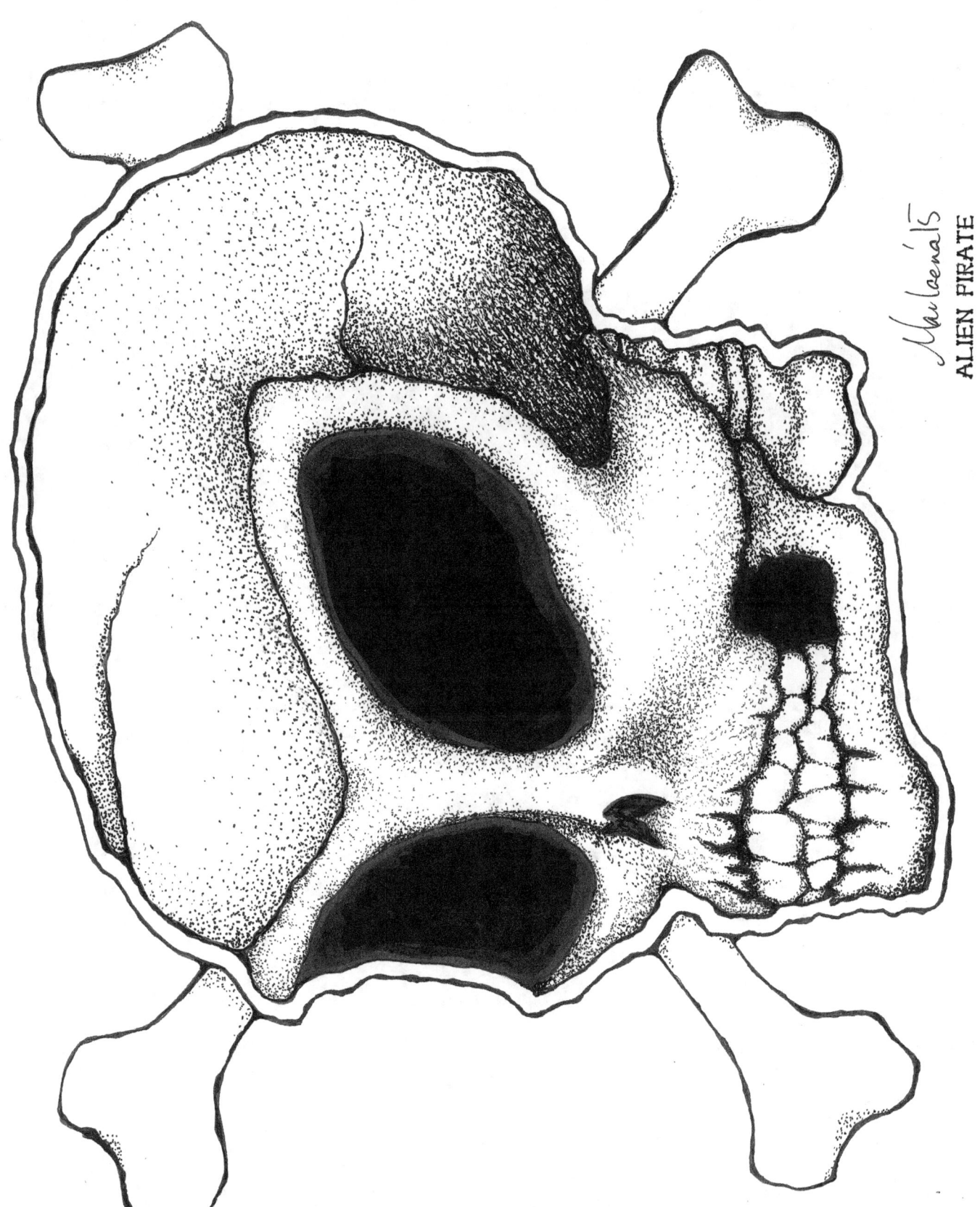

ALIEN PIRATE

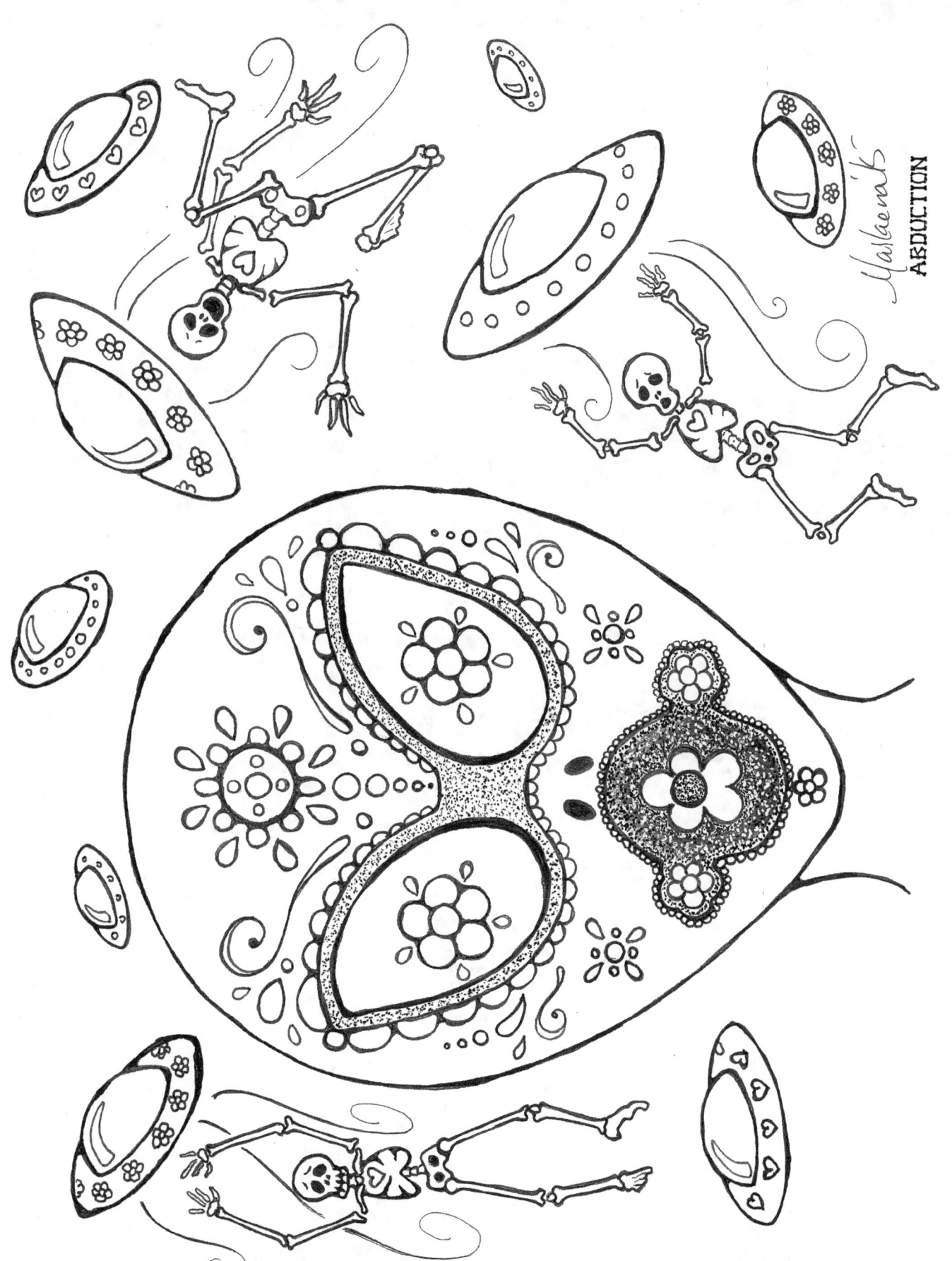

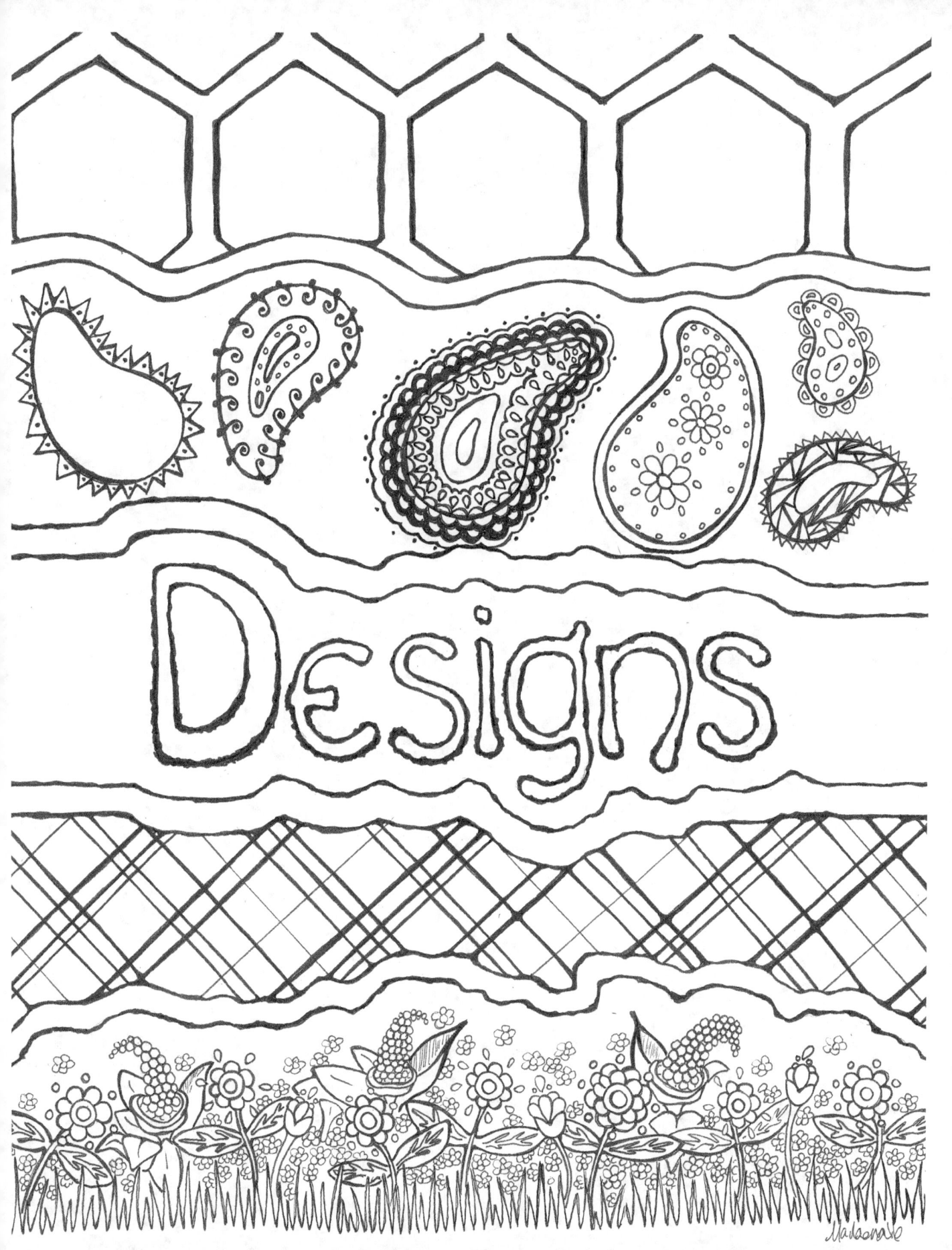

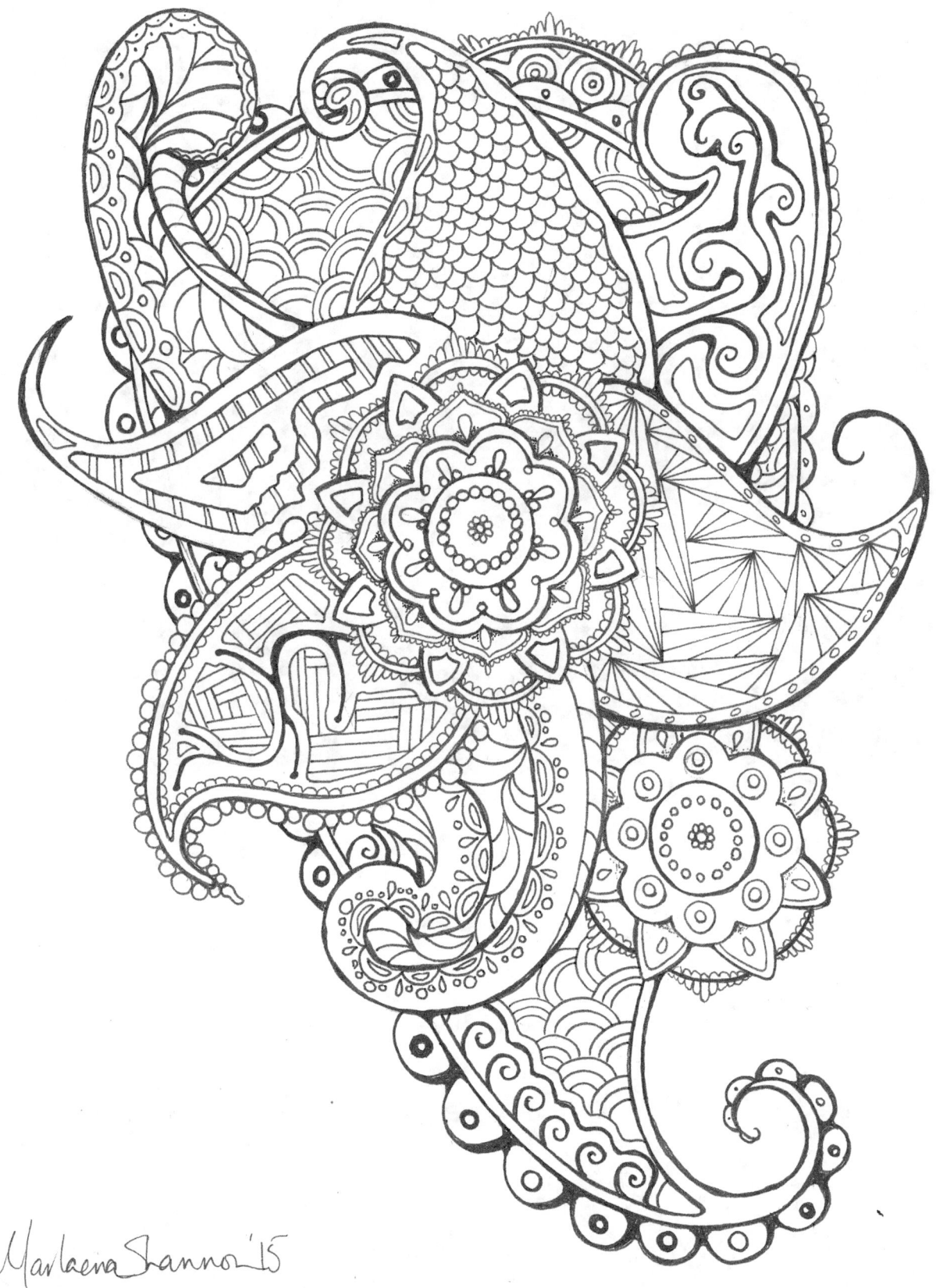

Marlaena Shannon '15

Star Trek Starfish

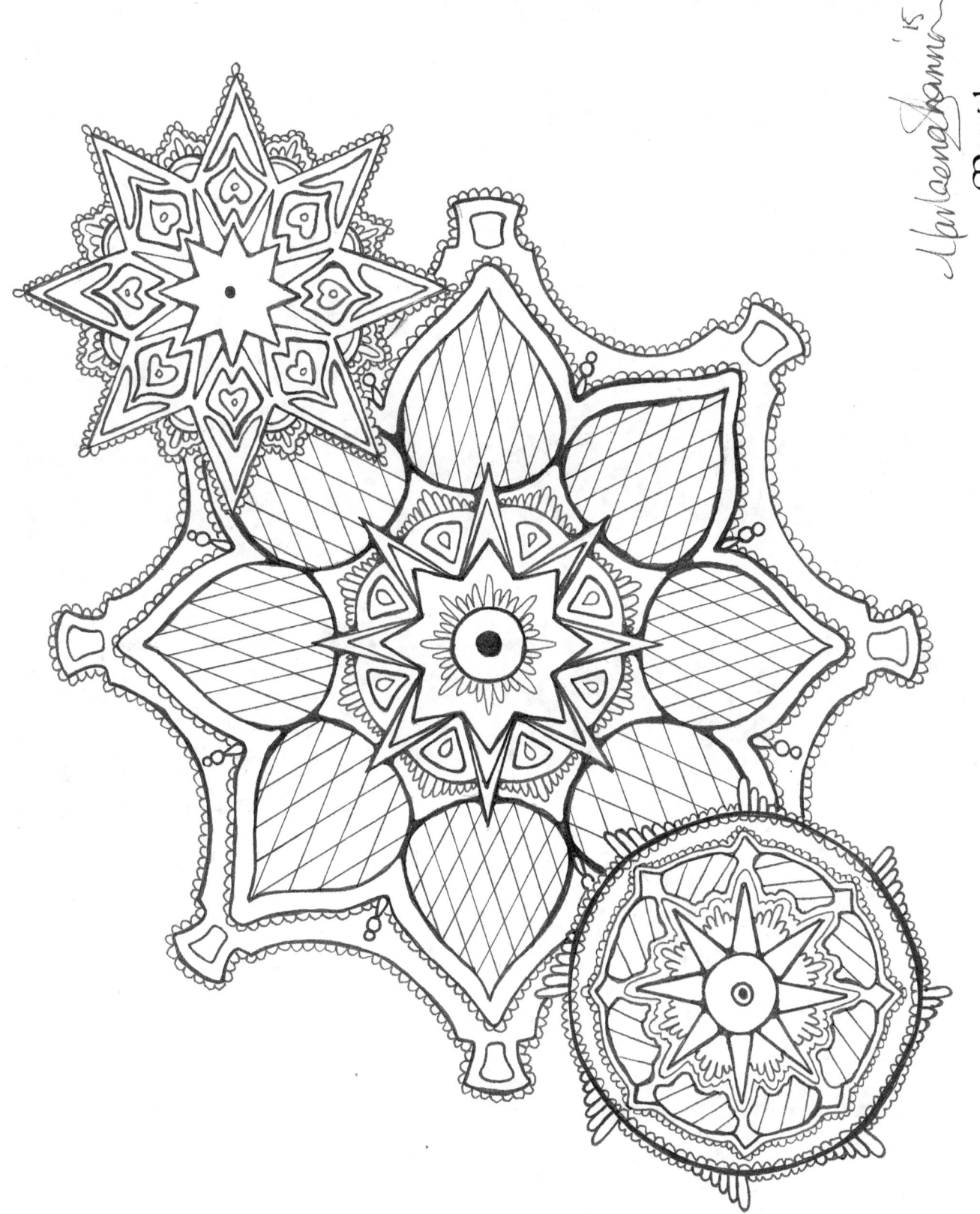

Marlaena Shannon '15
Moorish

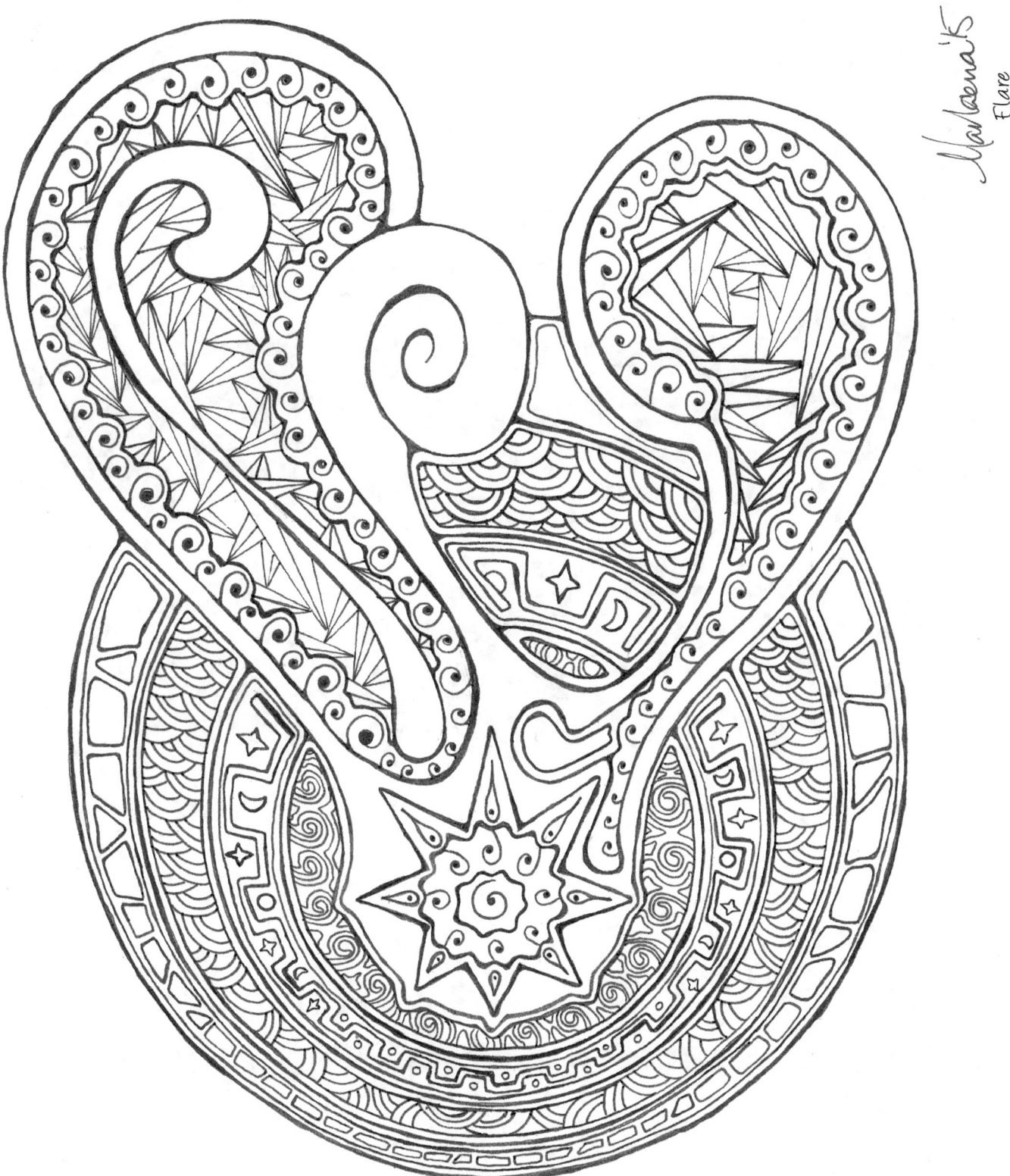

Marlaena's
Flare

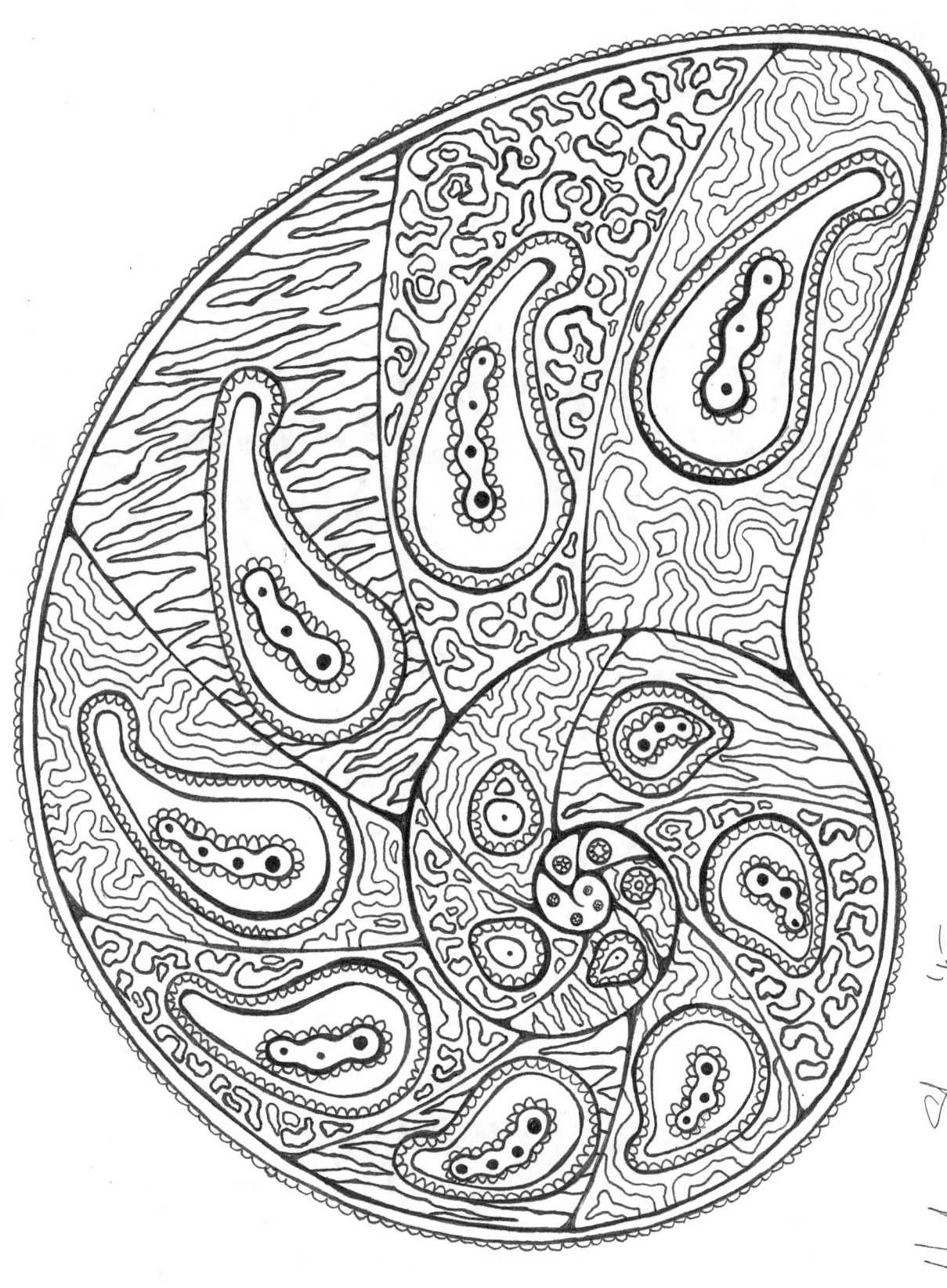

Malaena Shannon '15

Snail Makes Friends In the Jungle

Dahlias from BotanicaDivine.com

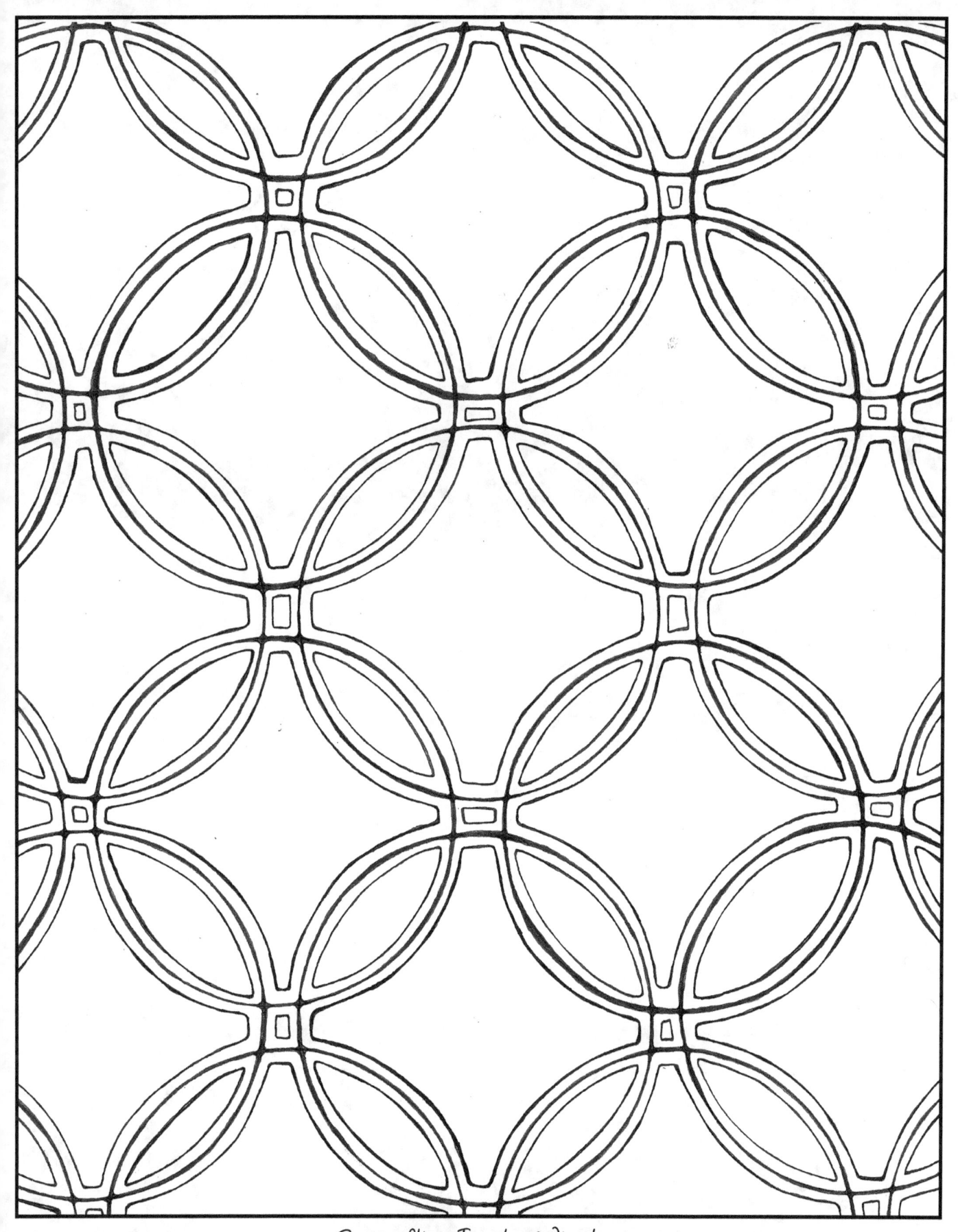

Butterflies In the Window

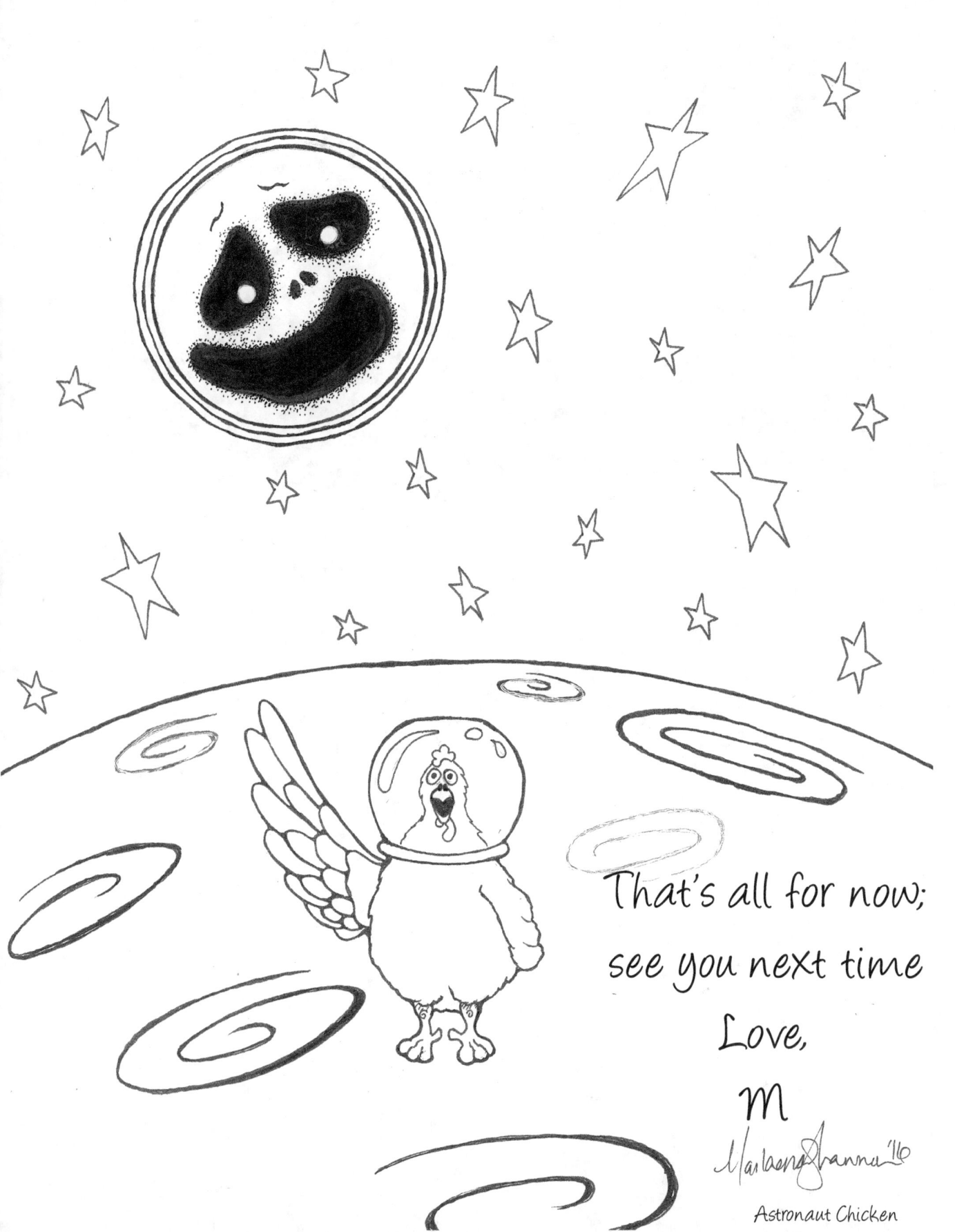

That's all for now;
see you next time
Love,
M

Astronaut Chicken